Go to the ant… consider its ways and be wise!

(Proverbs 6:6)

Reverent Jane

May you fulfil your purpose as the
Faith Resource that you are and
Come to take your place fully
as the 'Parent-healer' that
you have been called to be

Pastor Emmanuel Osi Eze (Author)
03/07/14

An environmentally friendly book printed and bound in England by
www.printondemand-worldwide.com

Mixed Sources
Product group from well-managed
forests, and other controlled sources
www.fsc.org Cert no. TT-COC-002641
© 1996 Forest Stewardship Council
FSC

PEFC Certified
This product is
from sustainably
managed forests
and controlled
sources
www.pefc.org
PEFC
PEFC/16-33-415

This book is made entirely of chain-of-custody materials

Faith Resources
The Emergence of a New Breed

– EMMANUEL OBI EZE –

London, UK

Readers are enjoined to share their experiences in practicing and applying the lessons, ideas and concepts in this book by emailing their thoughts to the author at: emmanueleze@powerhousecreators.com. Review comments can also be posted at www.powerhousecreators.com. All responses, review comments etc. will be most appreciated.

For worldwide distribution

Approbation

*F**irstly, may I congratulate you* (Pastor Emmanuel Eze) on a noble piece of literary work.

The topic 'Faith Resources', is off-piste in terms of mainstream Christian writing but is a key and necessary ingredient in helping us to be focused and aligned in our mission as servants of the Most High God.

I found that the book was drawing me in... to the extent that I didn't want it to finish...

Andrew Junaid
Senior Pastor,
Brook Lane Community Church,
Bromley, UK

Dedication

F irstly, to God Almighty who makes all things possible – God my Teacher who worked in, with, through, for and even despite me; in bringing this book to fruition. The same God, I trust, who will no doubt continue to work even beyond me, to stir, wrought[1] and give birth to even greater fruits by and through this book! I owe Him my entire life.

Secondly, to all parents (biological and spiritual) who constantly play tremendous roles in the strides of many destinies – including mine! Especially the rare few, who have managed to master the learned wisdom of erasing (by the Spirit) all lines between biological and spiritual, by fusing both so well.

Finally, to all those who genuinely and honestly wish to satisfy the greatest cry of the human spirit, "Who am I? Why am I here?" and genuinely aspire, and will strive, to emerge a new breed of Christians – Faith Resources!

---

[1] Although this may not make much grammatical sense it indeed makes sound theological sense. The sense in which I understand the word wrought to have been used in the Bible and the same sense in which I have sought to use the word here is to show that from the very beginning, God already crafted/made all things with delicate care ("Intelligent Design") but we only see their physical manifestation in due time as preset by God Himself - the Creator of all things created. He has made us (humans) in His image as "creators" to bring about this physical manifestation in our realm. So that whatever is "created" was not just created at the time it was physically made but only a physical manifestation of that which already preexisted in the spirit realm.

Acknowledgements

I **will be somewhat presumptuous** if I fail to acknowledge and appreciate the fact that I have come through very significant and challenging points to reach this stage in my life, because of the abundant grace and mercy which God has for me. The least I could say is, 'Thank you Father'. I pray I will never lose sight of your loving kindness and loving forgiveness.

Though there is an endless list of people who have helped shape who I am today, functioned as destiny helpers (even in giving birth to this book) - and together shared my days of joy and sadness, active and dull moments, humbleness and exaltation, work and loneliness, humours etc… and all the laughter that came with them. I doubt if my life would have amounted to much or if I would be the person that I am today, without this beautiful tapestry of people that God has so graciously blessed me with. I must confess that their generosity to me cannot be compromised nor overemphasised. Though I am unable to individually acknowledge them all here, they no doubt know who they are and heaven bears record. However, I must mention a handful:

My profound appreciation goes to the love of my life and my "mummy" (Pastor Jacqueline Eze) and our beautiful princesses (Jerusha and Jedidah) for their love, sacrifices and unflinching spiritual, moral and emotional support. Also, for according me the time and space necessary to complete this work.

Immense gratitude to my parents for modeling for me true parent-leadership: Papa and Mama Eze, Mummy and Daddy Israel Abam and Daddy Emmanuel Anyakwo (who sadly passed away a few years ago but his memory and profound examples still live with me) and Mummy Anyakwo: Thanks for being there when it really mattered.

I am also thankful to Mummy & Daddy Wale Adefarasin for the roles they played in helping to shape my destiny. You will always have a special place in my heart.

Reverend & Mrs Mills, for being such true friends and family. In you guys I have found Scripture to be true: that indeed "…there is a friend who sticks closer than a brother."[2]

My fellow pastors in Bromley (Jonathan McGill, John Ingle, Jonnie Horner, Martin Bredemear, Andrew Junaid, Russell Chadwick, Israel Oyebamiji, Emmanuel Ediale etc.) for their fervent prayers, friendship and firm support.

All our precious sons and daughters at TGL Church – who have so graciously accorded us the privilege of being parent-leaders to them. Thank you for your love, support, prayers and goodwill.

Jane Wade for your patience and for working so hard on all the graphics.

Mark Plummer for such patience and yet professional guidance.

_____

[2] Proverbs 18:24

Marika Buttigieg of Printondemand worldwide for going beyond duty's call; in patiently and painstakingly coordinating the entire proofreading and printing processes. Your passion and expertise has been a source of strength and encouragement for me and I consider you one of my destiny helpers. I pray that God will richly bless and send you your own destiny helpers also!

Many thanks to all those who, in spite of their impossible schedules, still took the time to read the pre-proof copy and send me their outstanding review comments. May our good Lord redeem and even hold time still for you and abundantly reward your great labour of love. Worthy of particular note here is Rev.Dr. Roger Standing, for also endorsing this pioneering work.

Reverend Israel Olofinjana, Reverend Eric Mills, Apostle Israel Abam and Pastor Andrew Junaid (who actually sacrificed part of his holiday) for taking the time to read and comment on the manuscript.

I also would like to particularly acknowledge my friend and brother Azuka 'Zuke' Obi, whose recent book release *The Power to Excel – Reaching For Your Best* really encouraged and inspired me, in an uncanny way, to dust up my manuscript and complete this book! Thanks coach Zubby!

Reviews and Comments

"First may I congratulate you and give honour to God for giving you the courage and insight to produce such a Kingdom resource.

The front Cover

As a visual person, the front cover's images intrigued me, I wanted to understand why the images were used. It is only when you Start reading the book that one understands the use of the imagery.

Content

The book is easy to read and is very in depth. It is a resource in itself and the style of writing reaches multiple audiences. The topic raised is very interesting and is a great resource for Leadership and Personal Development. Great insights and is very much thought-provoking. Like the use of insects and the comparisons given. Helps the reader to reflect and consider their purpose, which is much needed in the Kingdom - Great to have questions to cause reader to reflect on personal growth.

Thank you - Look forward to having a copy on our bookshelf amongst the other resources we have drawn from for personal growth.

God Bless you"

Bishop Llewelyn Graham, National Overseer (Atg), and **Pastor Susan Graham**, National Children and Youth Ministries Director - Church of God of Prophecy (CoGoP).

"The book has been well written, easy to read and straight forward. So, understanding or grasping the key themes of the book should not be hard for the reader. The purpose of the book in ministering and provoking the reader to personal reflection is achieved from the onset. At certain points I found myself challenging, celebrating and reflecting on the author's points of view/perspective as suggestive remarks were made about the subjects of Spiritual Parenting, Parent-Leadership, Faith Resources and the Church. Bringing me to the conclusion that, beyond the author, these points are relevant (not just) within the church today (but also for all Christians in all contexts!). Faith Resources: This concept is refreshing, true and edifying! All in one! Before this book I had never heard of nor read about the term. Now, I reflect on the state of my faith not as a means to an end, but as a living resource."

Shola Ekperigin

Director, The GTC Group (www.thegtcgroup.com)

"Evidently a lot of time and effort has gone into this work, for which it is commendable. It possesses depth of material which is a strength..."

Miscellaneous

Endorsement

"Pastor Emmanuel is keen for the body of Christ to know the 'faith resources' provided by 'parent-leaders' who help every believer to grow to be like Jesus. May his vision be a reality within the body of Christ in these days."

Revd Dr Roger Standing, Principal of Spurgeon's College, London

Contents

Foreword

The issue of spiritual parenting and leadership is a phenomenon that transcends rhetoric and calls for more effective approach and consideration. It is one of the most disturbing issues in the Body of Christ as the lack of 'real' spiritual parents and leaders creates an opportunity for the enemy of our souls to injure, cut down and decimate mercilessly believers that would easily have become "Faith Resources" to advance not just the message of the Kingdom but the Kingdom itself. A cry for spiritual parents and leaders is therefore a cry that easily resonates across the entire spectrum of our faith.

Some of us seem peculiarly to have been privileged to have enjoyed a high level of spiritual parenting and have become, by the grace of God, what we are today in the Body of Christ – "Faith Resources" – as a result. The desire that such spiritual parenting as we have been privileged to enjoy becomes the common experience of every true believer makes us strongly recommend this timely and riveting piece of inspiration to all.

One thing is clear: no one approaching this book with an open conscience would ever remain unhealed. The reason is simple. By the inspiration of the Holy Spirit, our greatest Teacher, Pastor Emmanuel has tactfully resolved many longstanding confusions of faith in God, banished the fear of being vulnerable before others, skilfully unwrapped the scepticism of open and intimate relationship between spiritual parents and sons or daughters and had clearly taught that we all fail if we do not lovingly and painstakingly pass onto others what we have been given by God for the furtherance of His Kingdom.

Read this book and become a "Faith Resource" or a better one at that!

Israel W. Abam.
Senior Pastor
Guiding Light Assembly,
Abuja Worship Centre.
Nigeria.

Introduction
(Opening Words)

*T**he premise for this book*** is the priesthood of all
believers[3]; whereby its intent is to speak to all
Christians, especially those called to various leadership
positions, irrespective of the context in which they lead –
church environment, corporate or political arenas,
academic or social circles etc. The truth elements and
principles in this book are intended to be cross-context and
transferable. A compendium of sorts, attempting to
highlight some critical propositions that are vitally
instructive for every Faith Resource that wills to emerge as
a new breed. Thus, every leaning towards any form of
Nicolaitans[4] spirit or mentality that has become so common
in leadership today – especially in our churches - is
deliberately and frantically avoided.

The idea is not to write a new book on parenting and/or
leadership, per se, as there are many excellent authors on
these subjects already. However, the intention is to draw on
some of the many existing excellent materials and propose
an all-important correlation between parenting and
leadership that has thus far never really been drawn nor
really practiced.

---

[3] In the context of 1 Peter 2:5, 9 per MSG & NIV translations
[4] The word *Nicolaitans* means "conquer the people" (See Revelations
2:6; Wiersbe, 847). Apparently a group in the church lorded it over the
people and promoted a separation of "clergy" and "laity" (see also Matt
21:20-27; 23:1-12)

In approaching this seemingly simple and straightforward, "two-word" subject; I interestingly found it quite intricate, hugely complex and almost elusive; but yet somewhat addictively engaging! I quickly realised I was possibly treading on what might be a relatively new dimension of Christian thinking and endeavour, and thus offer the pioneering work of this book as my own little contribution to this seemingly new dimension of Christian thinking.

Expected Learning Outcomes
(Focus & Purpose of the Book)

In dealing with the subject at hand I hope to spark some conscious realisation of the fact that every Christian is a leader and parent of sort; thus engendering the building of a generation of *Christian leaders* in every child of God, as crucial Faith Resources for the Church, our nation, time, context and ultimately for the Kingdom.

Therefore, some of the outcomes expected include, but are not necessarily limited to:

1.   Challenge, inspire and stimulate us as leaders, with certain critical thought processes and hopefully provoke specific action to further studies, research and, ultimately, firm action at higher levels of service and servant leadership. This new level is what I have termed Parent-Leadership.

2.   Aid the discovery of deeper levels of purposes and destinies here on earth and provoke deeper and more conscious considerations of our higher destinies beyond the here and now; with permanent cognisance "...of him to whom we must give account."[5]

3.   Ultimately help engender major shifts in our mind-sets, focus and priorities in our walk with and work for God - from any iota or shadow of narrow-mindedness - to a more large-hearted selflessness in leadership.

---

[5] Hebrews 4:13

Hopefully, provoking the resolve to be "good" leaders in all circumstances; worthy of God's ultimate approval.

4.   Make Christians aware and/or reinforce the fact that we are meant to be leaders in our various spheres of influence, irrespective of the size or extent of that sphere (be it at home, amongst our peers, at work, or at broader levels: economy, politics, academics, church etc.).

5.   Hopefully ignite a new passion to maximise and bring such influence(s) to bear beyond our own immediate local settings; bringing our weights to bear on our national life as well.

6.   Highlight the fundamental truth that our true leadership potential(s) as Christians and benefit to our communities and nation cannot be fully realised unless we submit to God; not just by being "born-again" but, crucially, by carrying and reflecting the *full image of God*. It is important to note here that especially as men/women and Christian leaders, we bear the *IMAGE OF GOD*.

7.   Drive home the revelation that we are an embodiment of resources/seeds and therefore not just Faith Resources, but *"RESOURCE-FUL(L)"*! (i.e. we are full of resources!), thus provoking the desire as well as opening up critical thought-patterns for fruitfulness.

8.   Highlight and make Christians more aware of our spiritual resources (i.e. the believer's wealth in Christ). Ephesians 1-3 describe where these resources come from – relationship with Christ and our position in Him; and Ephesians 3-6 encourages us to draw upon

those resources for our walk in Christ, a victorious Christian life and ultimately, translate these into tangible benefits for the Church as well as for our nation, and beyond.

9. Challenge those who have been called to parent (i.e.. father/mother) and nurture faith children (spiritually) to understanding that those children ought to be given the same attention, priorities and efforts as they would their own biological children and, I dare say, even more. To forge the understanding that if faith fathers/mothers really understand this critical need they would desire their biological children to also become their faith children and then ensure that there really shouldn't be any difference between both classifications – at least as far as standard needs for love, care and affection require.

10. Application is the ultimate outcome expected as a result of reading this book. We want to see our lives changed and transformed (beyond just the outward clothing of the Spirit's power to the all-important inward filling of the Spirit's life). We want to see a new breed of Christians emerge as Faith Resources – a distinctly different people who will be totally obedient to God and grow more like Jesus and reflect the full image of God – by applying the truth of this book to our own lives.

So you should be asking: how does this affect my relationship with God and those around me, in my sphere of influence? How does this affect me and my response to the enemy satan in whichever form he manifests? What is this book really saying to me; what does this mean and what am I going to do about what this book says and means?

As you work on applying the truth in this book to your life, I trust that God will bless your efforts to become "just like Jesus"[6] - by conforming you to the image of Jesus Christ – for this is the only condition for obtaining the promise... for "...This (peace, righteousness, security, triumph over opposition) is the heritage of the servants of the Lord (those in whom the ideal Servant of the Lord is reproduced)..."[7] Amen!

I have great expectations that God will wrought something deep and fresh in our lives even through this discourse and remain feverishly excited at the prospects that this book, in particular, portends. I hope you are too? Come with me!

---

[6] Max Lucado, 'Just Like Jesus' (Nashville: Word 1998), Keith Phillips, 'Discovering Truth – *Keys to Happier Living*' (Thailand: Aurora, 1999), Gene Edwards, 'A Tale of Three Kings – *A Study in Brokenness*' (Illinois: Tyndale, 1992) and Neil Anderson's 'Forgiving From the Heart' are some resources that have greatly helped me in this quest and I strongly recommend them as essential reading.

[7] Isaiah 54:17 (The Amplified Bible)

What's The Story?

*I*n *August 2011, I was* a key speaker at an international conference for pastors, leaders and workers, tagged 'Stewardship In Nation Building' and I was asked to deliver a lecture on the topic: Faith Resources. Following my lecture, I was overwhelmed by the response I received, as many participants requested my book on the topic! Sadly, I had no book for them at that point and quite simply offered copies of my lecture notes. The people challenged me to write a book on Faith Resources and that was the point at which the burden to expand and publish the idea was conceived.

As I nurtured the burden for this book, I realised that Faith Resources is beyond just a topic. For all its seeming grammatical structural simplicity, I found it packed with unfathomable convolution – a hugely complex conceptual phenomenon. I also discovered and indeed, in my opinion, consider this to be a somewhat new, but equally fascinatingly intriguing dimension in the field of Christian thinking and academic endeavors.

Over the course of the last two and a half years or so, since August 2011, I have grappled with and given much reflective thoughts and considerations to the different dimensions of this subject. By divine orchestration, I, within that period, also (somewhat uncannily) stumbled on some profoundly relevant and challenging materials at every juncture that I experienced some serious and mind-boggling emotional and experiential bewilderment - within myself, as dished by others to me and also, I reckon, inadvertently dished by me to others as well! All these and more helped me to develop and shape the snippets of my experiences and bursts of insights that I have shared in this book – I reckon, only as a starter to a much broader conversation!

Background

In his book *Building A Stronger Economy – My Dream For My Country.*[8] Christian Wogu (Africa's leading corporate systems specialist, renowned lawyer, activist and Nigeria's Presidential aspirant) has written some thought-provoking chapters. But the ones on 'Faith Resources' & 'Making Your Signature Count' struck some resonating chords for me. Playing around with such concepts as "Faith Resources", "spiritual resources" and "religious resources" etc. Wogu tries to emphasise the enormity of the contributions to the Nigerian national life of faith groups as a whole and the Church in particular.

Citing landmark institutions, systems and legacies that have been built by Christian leaders; using their personal skills, influence and the enormous pool of common wealth of the Church (human capital and financial resources etc.), he insightfully makes the connection and argues the possible extension of such achievements for the common good of Nigeria as a whole.

In making the valid connection between "priesthood" and "nationhood", he argues for and suggests that Christian leaders be given the opportunity to transfer their ability to organise, build, achieve, generate wealth etc. in turning the nation of Nigeria around, and then return to "faith work" - although still maintaining relevant and much needed influence, continually, by being the "conscience of governance" - through instilling key Christian virtues and character elements like integrity, diligence, wisdom, faithfulness, holiness, righteousness etc.

---

[8] I would strongly recommend this book as essential reading

However, he creates critical balance by noting the sad state of the Church and the mind-boggling selfishness that rules the hearts of most religious "leaders". He boldly exposes the "reckless disregard" with which a lot of religious leaders enrich, entrench and even attempt to immortalise themselves at the expense of the people, thus creating in themselves religious monsters of sort! They have become so socially irresponsible that rather than empower their followers, they impoverish and violate them in many ways. He highlights some important points – words/phrases like attitudes, sacrifice, giving, character, care, empowerment, organisational culture and paradigm shifts as some necessary elements that such shameful leaders ought to give some deep consideration.

Wogu basically highlights how faith groups, using the enormous resources at their disposal, can, altogether, be harnessed and act as a veritable resource for nation building - if Christian leaders can adopt, imbibe and exhibit the right attitudes, character and perspectives.[9]

Furthermore, I was privileged to see, at the time, both the manuscript and the proof copy of the book: *Strides of Destiny – Lessons from the attitudes of Moses*[10]; where the author attempts to draw crucial lessons from the attitudes of Moses that made him succeed and fail as God's servant. Interestingly, I found the content of this book quite relevant to certain aspects of my lecture – both as essential

---

[9] Christian Wogu, 'Building A Stronger Economy – My Dream For My Country', (Lagos, Nigeria: El-TODA Ventures for Shechinah Resources, 2010), 184-208.

[10] NB: This book has since been published: Israel W. Abam. 'Strides of Destiny – *Lessons From The Attitudes of Moses*', (Abuja, Nigeria: LightGuide Publishing, 2011).

further reading, as well as an aid in unpacking those loaded aspects of my lecture at the time. The author's outline includes (1) Make your life count, (2) Sense of Destiny, (3) Training for Destiny,(4) Call of Destiny,(5) Strides of Destiny, (6) Destiny Helpers, (7) Enemies of Destiny, (8) Failed Destiny, (9) The Mercies of God, and (10) The Glory of Destiny. This is a masterful book by my spiritual father, Apostle Israel Abam, which I would strongly recommend as a must-read, as it would help your further studies and service your need to further unpack salient aspects of this book that we cannot possibly fully and conclusively delve into.

Insights received as I researched for my lecture, the challenges from my audience, subsequent deep personal experiences, reflections and studies, and as I thought further on these particular books, the Holy Spirit opened up fresh dimensions for me and thus the main idea for this book was conceived and here born!

Approach & Style

In my distinctive "reflective" preaching/teaching style, I have approached the task of this book by also asking and, hopefully, subtly provoking lots of questions in the hearts of my readers. Such questions are deliberately not all necessarily answered in the hope that I might challenge my audience to be like the Berean Christians (Acts 17:11). Consequently, my submissions in this book reflect my casual observations but, importantly, are also subtly anecdotal - being part of the result of my own personal experiences and depict elements of my own personal "faith journey" to the discovery of deeper purposes and destiny; I humbly invite your full and active participation and partaking in that journey.

Although my dominant style in this book is one of reflection and teaching, the nature of the subject and the complex themes demand a cocktail of styles. **My approach is also one of a deliberately curious style – not purely academic, not purely devotional and not purely testimonial.** Therefore, you may occasionally find me switching modes from teaching/lecture/seminar mode to preaching or bible scholarship and academic mode or down to even the crusader mode! You have to really brace yourself for this journey; the drive is fascinatingly intriguing!

Wogu's submissions are quite intricate and need a lot of unpacking for the average reader and my approach here is three-fold: (1) to attempt to, within the limits of time and space, unpack some very specific elements of Wogu's submissions, (2) to build on his excellent work in this novel area of Christian thinking, and then (3) to attempt to extend these lines of Christian thinking. I have played with very intriguing words, phrases and even concepts but refrain from pursuing a full etymological study. However, I urge that you endeavour to look at the Greek, Hebrew, Latin and French roots of the various words and I assure that you will be equally amazed, challenged and inspired as I was in my research for this book.

I strongly agree with Abam that one of the greatest enemies of destiny is "self". He gives strategies on the 'battle against the enemies within' which he describes as the battle of leadership as well as the 'battle against yourself' for you are your own chief enemy.

I therefore ask many pertinent questions like: What exactly is/are Faith Resources? Who are you? What are you? Whose are you? Where are you? Are you a noble seed? And so on. I have been able to discover and draw intriguingly insightful lessons from creatures like *cockroaches, ants, lizards, marmots, locusts* etc. Also, watch-out for the *cockroach phenomenon!*

"If there be therefore any consolation in Christ, if any comfort of love, if any fellowship of the Spirit, if any bowels and mercies... Let this mind (attitude) be in you, which was also in Christ Jesus:"
(Philippians 2:1,5 KJV)[11]

---

[11] NB: The nt:Sport Bible (NLT) reads Philippians 2:5 as follows, "Your attitude should be the same that Christ Jesus had."

Where Are The Parents?

*T**his is not just a*** rhetorical question but a sad reflection of reality. It unapologetically represents the heart's cry of multitudes across the entire spectrum of our Christian family. Scripture also laments: after all, even though we have ten thousand teachers/instructors (guides to direct us/guardians) in Christ, we do not have many fathers. "There are a lot of people around who can't wait to tell you what you've done wrong, but there aren't many fathers willing to take the time and effort to help you grow up..." As humans, we have, amongst other critical needs, a legitimate natural need and desire for significance, security, acceptance and even accountability. Scripture also holds some sort of two-edged assurance: "But also look ahead: I'm sending Elijah the prophet...He will convince parents to look after their children and children to look up to their parents. **If they refuse, I'll come and put the land under a curse.**" This turning and reconciliation of hearts is not one-sided but a two-way thing: estranged fathers to the "ungodly" children, and the rebellious children to the piety of their fathers. A reconciliation that is produced by repentance of the "ungodly" – the disobedient and incredulous and unpersuadable fathers and/or children to the wisdom of the upright in order to make ready for the Lord a people perfectly prepared in spirit.[12]

---

[12] See 1 Corinthians 4:15, Malachi 4:5-6, Luke 1:17, Mark 1:3 and Isaiah 40:3 (AMP, NIV, KJV & MSG)

The Restoration of Spiritual Fathering & Mothering is also a cry echoed by Larry Kreider. He highlights the fact that we indeed live in a fatherless/motherless generation (both naturally –in our homes- as well as spiritually – in the church as well as in all spheres of human endeavour) and thus such an incredible need for parents today. He proposes that the prophet Malachi's final words (Malachi 4:6) are now coming to pass in the sense that God is placing in the hearts of thousands of people across the world not just the deep desperate desire and heart's cry across the entire spectrum of the body of Christ; for spiritual fathers and mothers but also their willingness to become spiritual fathers and mothers. It is curiously fascinating to me that almost thirteen years after Kreider's book and without any prior knowledge of his book, that the Lord would place the burden for this book, independently, in my own heart. The Spirit of God is indeed at work!

Kreider goes on to give account of many - including pastors and other anointed and great men and women of God - he had encountered who still yearn for spiritual fathers in their lives as well as people who want to be spiritual fathers/mothers but don't quite know how to become such! He believes that the call of God in our lives not only entails that we become fathers and mothers but also includes a desire, by His grace, to give us spiritual fathers and mothers as we obey Him. Why is it important? People need anchoring, people need some roots and a sense of authentic relationship. All humanity is looking for authentic relationships and if there is anywhere authentic relationships can be found it should be in the church and amongst Christians at large. Someone to travel, laugh, cry, worship and pray etc. with you - in a father-child type relationship even before you "arrive"! The Lord desires to bless us with a great posterity, spiritually. But sadly, he despairs, the church seems more concerned with having great events and programs than in fathering and mothering.

I believe that God wishes to change the way church looks by restoring fathers and mothers. Why send Elijah though? Because he is one prophet who seem to have understood what it means to be a true spiritual father. In that, upon the Lord's instruction, he found and took on Elisha as a son and they had such authentic father-son relationship in a spiritual parenting bond and from the moment he threw his mantle upon Elisha, everywhere you saw Elijah, you also saw Elisha even if no other members of the school of 50 or so prophets was there Elisha was always with him to the extent that when Elijah was taken up, Elisha didn't cry and address him as "great prophet" which he was or anything like that, but here is what Elisha cried: "...My father, my father..." (2 Kings 2:12). This unequivocally confirms that even though they didn't know each other before nor were they biologically connected, they had truly become one family!

Q: Do you hear the cry of a multitude of fatherless and motherless children in desperate need for their spiritual parents today? Will you respond, restore harmony, pour your life and impart your inheritance into your spiritual children? But who is this Elijah? Has he come or is he still to come? Was this promise fulfilled through Jesus Christ, wherefore we are to simply "put on Christ"[1] and let the same mind be in us that was in Him?

Now it is crucial to note that Spiritual fathering and mothering has nothing to do with age but everything to do with obedience. You can't give what you don't have: so spiritual parents ought to have spiritual parents themselves but must also be secure in the Father's love.[14]

New breeds! What happened to the old?

For there to be a breed at all there must be a brood. A new breed infers and indeed requires a new (different) brood. This new breed does not despise the old but rather strengthens, complements and challenges them to renew (Romans 12:2) and come up higher.

This new thing also requires new ways of parenting based on a new mindset - the mind of Christ. Parents that are indeed mindful of the encouragement, comfort, fellowship, tenderness and compassion that they've also enjoyed from Christ and the fellowship of His Spirit. This love that made a difference in their own lives and to whom being in a community of the Spirit means something - they have a heart for and do really understand, care about, and genuinely seek and pursue the realization and attainment of their faith children's callings and destinies. [15]

So, we start by joining the songwriter in asking: Where are the fathers (and mothers)[1], the responsible ones?

---

[14] Larry Kreider, 'The Cry For Spiritual Fathers & Mothers', (Ephrata, Pennsylvania: House to House Publications, 2000).NB: At the final printing stages of this book, I, quite interestingly, stumbled on this delightfully poignant and relevantly and simply indispensable book by larry Kreider and thankfully was able to catch the printers just in time to include some of his arguments here!

[15] See Philippians 2:1 (NIV & MSG translations)

Lessons From Personal Experience

*R*elatively recently, I went through such a bewildering experience which involved one of the couples that I had come to confidently regard and hold highly in esteem as one of my faith parents: a couple to whom I willingly and happily submitted not just myself and ministry but also my entire family and all that concerned me.

I believe that God's set order in the process of erring-forgiveness-restoration is that when the sinner repents and turns to Christ by faith, God shows mercy and grants pardon. Therefore, in our interrelationships, the errant person must first repent (unfeigned) and actively seek forgiveness and restoration. In line with the principles of this set order, I tried to reason with and explain things to them, forgave and asked forgiveness for any hurt (whether real or imagined on both sides). Although they assured me that it was one big unfortunate misunderstanding and that all was now well, their drastic change in attitude (one that clearly seems like complete aloofness) was most disturbing.

Although we still consider that they, in many ways, were somehow and (I choose to believe) continue, in many ways (unseen?), to be amazing parents to us and we believe to many others also, I had still always longed for something more and felt that they could be far more involved, caring and attentive parents to me and my family than they were or perhaps prepared to be. To me (and my family), this relationship had, in many ways, always felt too fragile and one-sided as well as shallow, devoid of the depth and level of spiritual substance that we sought, desired and longed for and thus simply lacking in complete fulfilment. Therefore, I guess it's not difficult to imagine or see the total shock and bewilderment that their new attitude and disposition left us in! Could it be that our expectations were just too high? Were we just asking for something that they quite simply didn't have the capacity to give? Are there any other faith-parents that are doing for their children what we are asking of ours or are our expectations simply unreasonable and/or unattainable?

Now, my reasoning and perception was that this whole episode surrounded and impacted an important stride towards my destiny. In fact, the whole confusion delayed and even threatened to completely abort a critical stage in my walk with and work for God. In spite of this, I was so stunned that they (in my own perception, reading and estimation) seemed highly insensitive and uninterested and showed such reluctance to address the matter with the required necessary and appropriate dispatch.

I was in turmoil within myself. I actually saw sides of me that I either never knew existed or simply did not think were still there. I sought answers to so many questions; but questions simply begat questions! I found myself going through a strange myriad of emotions - from dismissing them with the conclusion that their parenthood over me was all a big mistake in the first place; to the realms of hatred, bitterness and unforgiveness... I just felt really messed up and it felt like I had been bereaved!

However, one thing that helped me through this and helped me heal completely, was the fact that I had understood very early in my strides of destiny that: leadership is accompanied by wounds, offences and pain, but I cannot allow the wounds of leadership to develop into what some have termed spiritual "woundedness" or indeed allow it to discolour my attitude.[17] I also thank God that I have another couple who have also been true parents (having proven many times over to be our assigned "destiny helpers" not just for short segments but for the whole of our faith journey![18]). They helped my family and I through this exceptionally difficult time, just as they had consistently and unwaveringly done many times before - at every crucial point of our strides of destiny.

I learnt many things through that experience and the ensuing schooling/learning process. I sincerely hope that I can share a few of these lessons within the confines of this book.

A New Approach: "Faith-Resource-Parenting" & "Parent-Leadership"

Parenting in modern-day Christianity appears to have been degraded to mere mentoring! Worse still, the western mindset surrounding this new trend and development seems to also suggest that a fee ought to be attached to such "service"!

However, I believe that when God created parents, He made a perfect blend. A guardian and protector, a mentor and a friend... someone to guide your footsteps along the path of life, an ally to be at your side in times of tears and strife... God gave their loving arms the strength for any

---

[17] There is a whole teaching on Spiritual Woundedness by Mark Daniel and John Mulinde of World Trumpet Mission. Also see DH Mills' Art of Leadership (p.110)

[18] Abam, 43-48

task so they could help to clarify, test, approve[19] and ultimately fulfil the godly dreams which their dear child(ren) might ask or carry. This was what I expected from my faith parents in my dire moment of madness and the ensuing crisis. Unfortunately, some came far too short of this expectation and I was tempted many times to give back the same attitudes and nuances as I was getting; but the nagging question: 'does a child ever cease to be a child or a parent ever cease from being a parent – did God make such relationship revocable at will?' kept me from such fatally drastic action. 'Once a son, always a son!' became my guiding principle and conversely, 'once a parent always a parent!' should equally guide those who hold themselves out as faith parents. I came to the conclusion that, because I am willing and obedient to God's commands, I will keep living out the principles of love, respect, honour and enduring devotion (even if not mutual nor reciprocated); to do otherwise would run directly contrary to the mind (attitude) of Christ and indeed negate the principal essence of the love of God which fails not.

Dr (Mrs.) Nkem Okoro (a true mother in Israel) has written a very powerful book on parenting[20] and I believe that, whilst she focuses on the natural biological family system, the truth that she reveals runs in tandem and can and really should be seen to be applied within the spiritual family of God's people. A good relationship requires interaction filled with mutual love, respect, honour and enduring devotion to one another. Unfortunately, however, this is not the case. In fact, it seems to me (based

---

[19] See Romans 12:2b
[20] Nkem Okoro, 'Grooming The Next Generation: Effective Parenting and Mentoring of Children' (Lagos, Nigeria: Henriz Designs, 2010).

on casual observation) that a vast number of people that are regarded as fathers and mothers in the faith may not appear to really know nor understand what it really means to be parents to spiritual children.

Casual observations would show that parenting has literally been reduced to merely "mentoring" and many people (especially those of western culture and heritage) see fathering, mothering, coaching, mentoring (or what have you) as some form of "service", enterprise or even money-making scheme where their faith children have to register with them, pay periodic homage, fees and even tithe to them! These children in turn receive periodic letters or at most "review" meetings. Unfortunately, this warped concept of spiritual "parenting" seems to be permeating many other cultures and societies too.

In my humble opinion, from casual observation, many of these so-called parents (to whom it would seem the description or idea of being a faith father/mother has become mere status symbol) are prepared to stick with their biological children no matter how messed up they may be – they pray, support and hold out hope that they would somehow turn out right. However, the slightest "error" by their so-called faith/spiritual children; and they hold them at arm's length or even cut them off completely.[21] The simple truth and reality is that a parent never ceases to be a parent and a child never ceases to be a child to their parents,

---

[21] I am aware that, sometimes, and in some cases, it is the faith parents that suffer this treachery in the hands of their so-called faith children. But we here focus on the first instance. Although specifics of each situation/case ought to be assessed on its own merit, the general principles here expressed universally apply – regardless of whose perspective is being viewed.

regardless. So, surely, I would have thought that faith/spiritual children are to be treated with the same love, care and support as biological children rather than the current unhealthy and rather faulty understanding and discriminatory treatment that I see all over the place. The lines between biological and spirit ought to be cleared by the Spirit. Indeed, the ideal would be for biological children to also become spiritual/faith children in order to fully enjoy all the dimensions of the ideal parent-child relationship. Indeed our mutual obedience to and fellowship in God is thicker than blood for it erases our various biological bloodlines giving us a common bloodline – the blood of Christ![22]

Little wonder why the song writer asks, "where are the fathers (parents)… the responsible ones?" Thus, for a new breed of Christians - Faith Resources - to emerge, we must get back to basics and understand parenting and being parented, in turn, within the family of God's people - learning from how God relates to us as His children, the orders and examples that He has set in nature as a whole, and how we must imitate this; our forbearing approaches and attitudes to our biological families etc… and then transfer these as prototypes of sorts to our faith family – with '…bowels of mercies'![23] This faith family system requires all parties to firmly understand this fundamental truth: someone has heard what you have not; been places you have not (or perhaps never need to go); seen what you have not; knows what you do not. Your success in fulfilling your entire destiny also depends on your willingness to be parented, just as you are parenting.

---

[22] See Ephesians 3:15 (NIV) & Mark 3:33-35 (MSG).
[23] Colossians 3:12 KJV

Faith parents, as God's chosen people, must therefore clothe themselves with compassion, kindness, humility, quiet strength, discipline, gentleness and patience. They must be even-tempered, willing and quick to grant complete absolution when repentant children ask forgiveness with genuine brokenness and contrition - as the Lord forgave them- and over all these virtues put on love, which binds them together in perfect unity.[24] This is the order of God, the example He shows and the lesson He expects that parents teach by their very own conduct.

God Our Teacher[25] - *The Schooling Process*

This new breed of Christians that will operate as true Faith Resources can, therefore, only emerge as a result of a major paradigm shift. This shift will entail parents who, as bishops of many great destinies, are '…apt to teach…' cool, collected, accessible, attentive to their children and commanding their respect[26] - having themselves being taught by other parents and ultimately so by God our master teacher. Parents who are, themselves, Faith Resources and can teach and replicate themselves as their children seek to be imitators of God.

Faith children ought to be able to clearly watch and see what God does in, with, through and for their faith parents and then do and experience the same, like children who learn proper behavior from their parents.[27] Faith parents

---

[24] See Colossians 3:12-14 (NIV & MSG)
[25] See: Robert W. Pazmino, 'God Our Teacher – *Theological Basis in Christian Education',* (Grand Rapids: Baker Academic, 2001)
[26] See 1 Timothy 3:2-4 (NIV & MSG)
[27] Ephesians 5:1 (MSG)

must therefore be prepared, ready and willing to allow God to work despite and even beyond them to see their faith children emerge as even better and greater Faith Resources.

This new paradigm emphasises the need for grooming, guidance, training, mentoring, modelling and strategies for effective parenting (including active involvement and pursuing the most effective 'road map to destiny'). It also entails Faith Resource parents investing time in understanding their Faith Resource children's natures, unique needs, setting parental goals and providing physical, emotional, social and spiritual care, as well as good communication and effective discipline for the emerging Faith Resource who can, in turn, replicate themselves. This is an invaluable need for the emerging Faith Resources in their strides of destiny and to successfully navigate through the foreign and uncharted paths of life, overcome all the enemies of destiny and truly fulfill their call.

Therefore, Faith Resources are teachers who operate within a well-structured and established Christian family cum educational system – where God stands as the ultimate head-teacher. Thus, Faith Resources must possess, after the order of God's nature and examples, specific '...spiritual, mental, social and physical characteristics that are important qualifications for Christian teachers.'[28] There are also many other traits, features etc. that Faith Resources must bear and this book just attempts to begin a conversation - where these characteristics, traits, features etc. are not only highlighted but truly demanded of Christians (especially

---

[28] George R. Knight, 'Philosophy & Education – an introduction in Christian perspective' (Berrien Springs MI: Andrews University Press, 2006), p219-

faith parents and leaders); and actually lived out in the workings of our day-to-day dealings.

When this mind of Christ truly becomes our mindset, we will experience this much-needed paradigm shift. And that, my friends, will be the emergence of a new breed of Faith Resources!

I feel pressed to emphatically highlight at this juncture that the day we, as Christians, allow our *Christian distinctiveness*[29] to get blurred through compromise with the world around us, that day we cease being Faith Resources - no matter how *"resourceful"* we are or might be! Therefore, make sure you don't allow this to happen! Only then will you have a marked influence on those around you, starting with your family. The secret is in your *faithfulness in studying the Word*[30], *sustaining your prayer life, maintaining your integrity* and *prayerfully putting on our God-supplied armour on a daily basis.*[31] Did you know that Scripture actually shows God Himself putting on the armour (Isaiah 59:15-17), just as He (through the Apostle Paul in Ephesians 6:10-20) charges us to do? Wow!

What makes you distinct as a leader...?
Just the assertion that you are a Christian?
Reflect on this...

---

[29] As Christians (especially as leaders), we must portray this distinctiveness -particularly in the areas of integrity, habits, attitudes, character etc. as opposed to non-Christian leaders.
[30] See: 2 Timothy 2:15 (KJV) and Acts 17:11(NIV)
[31] Jim George, 'The Bare Bones Bible Handbook', (Oregon: Harvest House Publishers, 2006), 126; See also: Ephesians 6:10-20

Section Overview:

The big ideas here are those of Faith-Resource-Parenting and Parent-Leadership. Though the seemingly distinct roles of biological parenting versus faith parenting are, unfortunately and unhelpfully, usually kept separate; they really are one and the same role. Furthermore, the concept of parent-leadership proposes that leaders ought to be parents much in the same way that parents ought to be leaders. Faith Resources are those who have not only really merged the two roles effectively but also fully understand this is a lifelong commitment. Those who will fulfill not just the full roles of parenting as leaders but also lead as parents – also fulfilling, all at once, their roles as: visionaries, strategists, politicians, campaigners, coaches and change agents. The qualities required to effectively merge these roles into a seamless one are being honest, forward-looking, inspiring and competent.[32]

---

[32] Burt Nanus, Stephen M. Dobbs, *Leaders Who Make A Difference (Jossy-Bass Publishers, San Francisco, 1999).*

'Q: Just a few section closing reflective thoughts; for future development:

In view of mark 9:35ff, would you say that leadership (especially in ministry) is only for the charismatic or the "gifted" to be seen or called to such positions?

What would you say is the difference (if any) between God's calling and the fact that every Christian is supposed to be a leader of sorts?

Where does the mutual acceptance of both parties within a spiritual/faith parent-child relationship sit? How are the roles agreed and assumed? Do you think that we should shift from our present understanding – shrouded with unclear and confusing patterns – to a more standardized approach as a template for our universal Christian understanding of the structure/functions/roles/responsibilities etc of this critical relationships?

What is your opinion of those who never felt nor would ever feel the need to form any kind of spiritual parent-child bond with anyone? Or those who feel that mere mentoring or such largely detached relationships or even, indeed, "adequate" accountability and support network or arrangements is sufficient? Would you say that they are deviating from God's intended plan and order? Are they missing out on anything?

What patterns and examples for spiritual parent-child endorsement and relationships can we draw from Scripture?

Why is this practice not seemingly common place at present? Is it meant for everyone? Is it possible that this divine concept may have been misconstrued by many Christians (and non-Christians alike) as something totally different; and thus may have become or otherwise runs the risk of becoming another Christian cliché or another lingo in our so-called "Christianese" – where having a spiritual father or mother becomes akin to or similar in practice to the worldly order of having a "god father" or "god mother"?'

The Substance Of Faith
(What does it all mean?)

N *ow, I think it is* important for us to understand what Faith Resource really means, in order that we might fully appreciate, comprehend and perhaps even come to terms with our true nature as Faith Resources. To help us with this understanding, I have broken down the component parts of this all-important concept:

Faith:

The word faith in itself is a conceptual term that can be quite difficult to understand and has eluded the clear understanding of many! 'The Biblical concept of faith has been radically redefined in some philosophical and theological circles during the past century. Those definitions rarely address the complexities of the biblical concept, *a concept in which the whole person, the physical world, God's Word and God Himself play crucial roles.' There are objective and subjective characteristics* of biblical faith, which none of those alternative definitions are able to grasp.[33]

The words "faith", "trust" and "believe" in the Bible are all the same word in the original Greek. That's important to know because in English when you say you believe something, it, interestingly, doesn't carry the same connotation as to trust in something, does it? But faith is simply agreeing with something. When we understand this,

---

[33] *Holman's Illustrated Bible Dictionary*, (Nashville: Holman's Bible Publishers, 2003), 547 (bold and underline mine)

we can see that everyone/everything operates by faith and **even the atheist has "faith"**! So the question is not "do you have faith?" but rather "what is your faith in or on?" because faith is the reliance that you demonstrate by actions. No matter what we SAY, it's what we DO that shows what we really believe. So, if you want to know what you really believe, look at your actions – your daily choices, decisions, conducts, attitudes, words, deeds etc. *For no one can consistently behave in a way that is inconsistent with what he/she believes!*

Faith is <u>*confident trust in God*</u> and the salvation He provides in His Son Jesus, who is the only one that can save us from sin[34]. The Bible dedicates the whole of Hebrews 11 to define, describe and highlight the importance of faith in the life of anyone who desires to make a mark in life and leave their prints in the sands of time. Faith, it says, 'is the substance of things hoped for, the evidence of things not seen'. We see that Jesus is the '*author* and finisher of our faith', that God Himself operates by faith and consequently, by faith ONLY are we justified, truly successful and 'obtain a *good* report' from God (see Mathew 25:21 for the ultimate report that we must strive for).[35] Faith is the belief, trust and confidence in God and Jesus Christ and encompasses *"faithfulness"*[36]; which '...denotes *trustworthiness* or *dependability*'.[37] 'Throughout Scripture, faith is the trustful human response to God's self-revelation through His Word

---

[34] Ditto, 261
[35] Hebrews 11:1-40; 12:1-3
[36] William D. Mounce, *Mounce's Complete Dictionary of Old & New Testament Words,* (Michigan: Zondervan, 2006), 232
[37] *Holman's* 547.

and His actions… (and) denotes *reliability*, *stability* and *firmness*…'[38]

The Hebrew root word *Aman* concretely meant to support or to uphold, as for example **the strong arms of a parent would uphold an infant**. Those arms are sure, certain and firm.[39] So also the strong arms of good Christian leaders/parents are being awaited to uphold, not just faith children, but also our nation and indeed the world. The great theologian John Calvin defined faith as "a steady and certain knowledge of the Divine *benevolence* towards us…" I also agree with D.L. Moody that 'faith makes *all things possible*; *love* makes *all things easy*.' Faith is the *confidence in God* that leads to *obedience to God*. True faith is based on *what God says* and is *demonstrated in and by what we do* - our obedience! Remember, sin is simply disobedience – especially when we rebelliously seek to fulfil our (even legitimate) needs, in illegitimate ways. **People with faith do things for God in absolute obedience and God does things for them in absolute faithfulness.**"

James' challenge: 'show me your faith without works and I will show you my faith by what I do' (James 2:17-18) does not in any way contradict Paul's admonition in Ephesians 2:8-9 when he says we are saved (justified) by grace through faith and not of works lest anyone should boast. He is saying that if you really believe, it is going to affect what you do and what you say. Faith without action can range from one extreme of not taking any action at all to the foolishness of say, for instance: going to the airport with your suitcase wanting to go to London, finding out all

---

[38] Ditto
[39] Ditto, 548

about the flights times, (even all the technical details!), bought your tickets, gone through customs and immigration and now at the boarding gates – but never actually made a move to get on board the flight! The truth and reality is that people don't always live according to what they say they believe, but they will always live according to what they actually believe. For, indeed, no one can consistently behave in a way that is inconsistent with what he/she believes!

Now this concept is so complex that I can easily spend the whole time talking about it alone and still not finish, but I am conscious that it is only an element in our subject of discourse. Therefore, I must move on, but urge that we do our own further studies on this all-important and fundamentally profound biblical concept. However, it is my final submission, here, that *the suggestive reality that one can actually "lose" faith indicates the PRECIOUSNESS of this item of GOD'S GIFT. We are justified by faith and must live by faith (Habakkuk 2:4b)[40]. It is only by faith that we can truly 'make (our) word and… signature count'[41] and strategically position ourselves as Christian leaders – wherefore, we are subject to being upheld by God Himself and then become concretely relevant in firmly upholding not just ourselves, our families, but also, all those in our sphere(s) of influence(s) and, I dare say our nations and indeed the world!* See: Genesis 1:28.

---

[40] Though the Just shall live by faith, we also know that faith without works is dead **(James 2:14-26)**. We shall, hopefully, touch a bit more on this dimensions; in due course.

[41] Wogu, 242

Fear=Worry=Anxiety=Doubt

Ah, Fear! Of course we can't talk about faith without exposing the ever present danger and deception of fear which, on the other hand, is the direct opposite of faith - a great insult to our great and generous God. Unfortunately, so many "Christians" have come to almost, seemingly helplessly, succumb to a worldly mind-set by literally accepting the following thought pattern: *Living in a practical, cruel world it is "natural" that a lot should bother us e.g. being sinful – we fail; being prone to sickness – we hurt; being mortal – we die (in fact for many death or perhaps the fear of death seems to literally hunt them); pressures wear us down; anxiety gives us ulcers; people intimidate us (and we often succumb to such intimidation by being so oppressed and repressed to the extent that we allow such people, instead of God, to dictate to us what we can or cannot be or become!); criticisms offend us (even when constructive!). Diseases scare us* and the list is inexhaustible. In fact some of us may have allowed ourselves to be so hooked on worry that they even worry simply because there is nothing to worry about! However, we must bear in mind that these all result from sin - just as they are sinful in themselves! Matthew 6 warns us against worry. So, to worry or to be anxious is, in fact, sin!

Worry has been described as **"Interest paid on trouble before it comes due".** It is our worst enemy. Some statistics say that a great multitude of people now take pills to help them forget more worries about more things. Worry is fear driven and so, too, the direct opposite of faith. If you allow fear, through worry, to rule you; you will be very short on grace! **It's like a rocking chair, it requires a lot of energy and it gets you nowhere.** Leo Buscaglia said: **Worry never robs tomorrow of its sorrow, it only saps today of its joy"!** Dr

Charles Mayo says: ***"Worry affects the circulation of the whole nervous system. I've never known a man who died from overwork but I've known many who have died from doubt.*** Footballers, for instance, know this nervous-wreck experience all too well and the consequent failure/woeful performance that can often result when they come under the burden of expectation and allow fear/worry/anxiety to grip them. Professor Willie Rhilo (a football sports psychology expert) has termed this footballing experience "choking". This phenomenon is underlined by fear and doubt.

Doubt is simply double-mindedness[42] and always creates worry (which in itself is fear-driven). Lack of information further raises doubt. Anxiety and perhaps even depression are the ultimate results of this vicious cycle! The Solution, however, is simple: **do not worry about what you can't change and do not stress yourself complaining about what you've allowed!** There are more positive ways to use the energy that would have been wasted on anger, frustration, or worrying! So worry less, act more - for faith itself is expressed through positive action. After all faith without action, we are told, IS DEAD!

Faith vs. Fear

Our collective destiny is to become this new breed of Faith Resources. It is instructive to note that to emerge as a Faith Resource, faith is, not surprisingly, the only essential ingredient required. However, in the working out of this ingredient, there are bound to be many challenges and it

---

[42] See James 1:6-8. NB: David hated double-minded men (Psalm 119:113) and God declares such people unstable in all they do and assures that they will not receive anything from the Lord!

might even involve some wilderness experiences. Incidentally, in this stride of destiny, fear and the desire to return to the old (Egypt) remain an ever-present temptation.

The whole of Hebrews 11 is dedicated to this essential element. Faith, as we've seen, is confidence in God; that leads to obedience to God. True faith is based on what God says and is demonstrated by what we do. People with faith do things for God, and God does things for them. Faith is not a luxury; it is a necessity! It is for 'common' people as much as it is for great 'leaders'. We need faith for everything: worshipping (v4),; working (v7), walking (v8-9), waiting (v10-12), warring (v30-34) etc. Any area of our lives in which we ignore faith, we sin (see Romans 14:23)...

Q: Does Faith always entail an element of risk? Can Faith and Fear stand side-by-side in mutual co-existence? Can you have faith (I mean true faith) and still appear to be defeated or, worse still, be actually defeated?

Faith is strong unshakeable belief and confident trust in God, especially without proof or evidence and even when it seems unreasonable or irrational. *But can we live by faith and 'appear' to be defeated? Possibly!* Note that not everybody who trusted in God was delivered or protected (Hebrews 11: 35-40) **but the important thing is not God's deliverance; it's God's approval** (Hebrews 11:39).

The seasons of our lives will change every time we decide to use our faith[43]. Faith in God gives us the ability to continue, when others are giving up, faith makes all things possible, faith deepens our dedication to Christ, drives us to give service to His Church, reflects in the character and authenticity of our lives as Christians and manifests in our love for each other e.g. through hospitality and concern for one another. Such love makes it easy for us to be there for each other. This faith comes from first totally submitting to God, then committing to reading, studying, hearing and living the word of God (Romans 10:17 & 15:4). Without faith it is, indeed, simply impossible to please God. (Hebrews 11:6a). Faith in God gives us the ability to endure (and this, to my mind, includes bearing and forgiving each other's failings, errors, hurts, disappointments etc.) when others are giving up.

Fear, on the other hand, is directly contrary to faith. In Matthew 6:25-34, God particularly warns us against fear/worry/anxiety/doubt – a potent enemy of destiny that has indeed overcome many. Fear is the direct opposite of faith. It is a great insult to our generous, all-powerful and Almighty Heavenly Father - who, in His lavish and splendid goodness, has given us everything we need for life and godliness (2 Peter 1:3) and indeed richly provides us with everything for our enjoyment (1 Timothy 6:17) - that we even worry. When we are anxious or worry we are in disobedience of God's command and this is sin! What worries us masters us. Worry saps our energy and yields nothing in return (see Matthew 6:27).

---

[43] Mike Murdock, P.45

Because we live in a world filled with anxiety, it's easy to let it rub off on us, so that living in absolute faith - totally without worry - may sound impossible. Some of us may have allowed ourselves to be so hooked on worry that they even worry simply because there's nothing to worry about!

The fact that the Bible tells us not to worry about anything does not mean that these things don't matter. It doesn't mean we should fail to plan, project and organise our lives or that we should be reckless, complacent, lazy, shabby/tattered or anything like that. Far from it!

Jesus Himself enjoyed life to its fullest and wants us to have abundant life and enjoy the best of life. However, we are urged as followers of Christ to trust in God not in man, nor in material things, to put our money and resources to work for His Kingdom, to work hard, live simply and give generously, to help the needy and promote the gospel. Jesus does not deny the fact that money and other good pleasures of life make excellent servants, but warns that they can also make terrible masters, if we allow them.

Fear causes God huge amounts of pain. God only needs to be believed. His only pain is to be doubted. Put God first in absolute trust and you'll get the world thrown in. That's faith!

Why should you be weak, accept defeat, lack faith and wisdom to fulfil your destiny and calling or allow satan supremacy over your life through fear, worry, frets, confusion and even depression. Why should you say you can't by allowing ungodly pressures and expectations of life (including people pressures/ expectations, possession pressures/ expectations, performance pressures/expectations etc.) to bother you and make you feel discontented, worthless or even feel like a failure when the Bible says otherwise (See Psalm 27:1, Daniel 11:32, 2 Corinthians 2:14, Romans 12:3, 1 Corinthians 1:30, James 1:5, 1 John 4:4, 2 Timothy 1:7, 1 Peter 5:7, 1 Corinthians 14:33, 2:12, Lamentations 3:21-23, Philippians 4:13, John 16:33, Philippians 4:11, 2 Corinthians 5:21, Romans 8:37 etc.)? So, the Lord says to you today: be anxious for nothing! Will you believe and live this out? **To help you to begin working this out, please also see Philippians 4:6-9 and Ephesians 3:10 (particularly in the Message Translation).**

Sadly even the world seems to understand this better than us "Christians" and thus presents us with mathematical proof! An article by Zig Ziglar[44] States Dr. Mayo's findings: **Mathematically speaking, it really doesn't make sense to worry; or to be anxious, because Psychologists and much research tell us that roughly 40% of what we worry about will never happen and 30% of them have already happened. Additionally, 12% of our worries are over unfounded health concerns. Another 10% (or more - as some research say 18-20%) of our worries involve the daily miscellaneous fretting that accomplishes nothing (i.e. "sweating the small stuff")!** *That leaves zero (absolutely nothing!) to worry about. Just as the Bible says! Or, at best (or worse?), only 8%. So, even for those of us who love empirical proofs, we see that at least 92% of the time we worry for no good reason. But faith tells us that, by God's grace through Christ, even the 8% which the world would regard as perfectly good excuse to worry and be anxious is, alas, no reason at all!!*

So... what will it be? Faith OR fear/worry/anxiety/doubt? The CHOICE is yours!

_____

[44] ziglar.com (accessed 09/12/13)

Resource(s)

This, interestingly, also turns out to be an intriguing word. In fact, also more a concept than a word. The Collins English Dictionary offers about four very insightfully instructive understandings of this word:

1.   Capability, ingenuity, and initiative; quick-wittedness[45]; a man of resource

2.   A source of economic wealth, especially of a country (mineral, land, labour, (i.e. people) etc.) or (of a) business enterprise (capital, equipment, personnel (i.e. people), etc.)

3.   **A supply or source of aid or support; something resorted to in time of need.**

4.   A means of doing something; expedient (The French root *resource or resourdre* means *relief* or *to rise again;* the Latin root *resurgere* means *to rise*).

Q: I have to ask the following critically crucial questions: What do you resort to in time of your need, The Word, physical resources, money etc? Is the physical a means to an end or an end in itself? Is it secondary to the Word or vice-versa? Are people able to count on and depend on you for support when they repentantly need your understanding?

---

[45] Note that God is the one that gives us this quick-wittedness vis-à-vis the power of witty inventions - see Proverbs 8:12 (KJV)

I am urged at this point to speak into the lives of those needing relief, reprieve, respite, or any other form of Godly support in order to rise again. May those reading this now, who have never known what it means to be, or to become, let alone rise to the top and those who may have missed or tripped from the top, begin to rise and mount up with wings as eagles, may favour and understanding locate you today and may God grant you accelerated strides towards your destiny ... in Jesus's name! Amen!

Resourceful:

Ingenious, capable, and full of initiative (*"RESOURCEFULL?"*) especially in dealing with difficult situations.[46]

Faith Resources:

Having looked at the component parts of the phrase Faith Resources, I will attempt to construct a working definition of what this actually means for the purposes of our collective and general understanding. Whilst I understand and agree that there are many different kinds of resources; and whilst I also note that people often understand Faith Resources to be those items that help us build and sustain our faith (i.e. Bibles, Christian literatures

---

[46] Collins Softback English Dictionary, (Glasgow: HarperCollins Publishers, 1992), 1279

etc.), I urge a crucial paradigm shift in our overall understanding, and hereby offer this specific but purposeful understanding:

> Faith Resources are people (i.e. you and I)!
> (A very simple definition, but by no means simplistic).

Faith Resources are therefore men (and women of course!) who are born-again Christians, bear the full image of God and consequently are resourceful (i.e. full of certain essential "seeds" which reflect in their attitudes, form their character and ultimately distinguish them for "good" success and ultimate promotion. Such individuals are essentially marked for the creation and distribution of all sorts of powers and influence including, but not limited to, spiritual, social, political, religious and economic powers, as well as academic reformation and other wealth components. They are not just financial pillars in the Kingdom of God, they are ingeniously strong arms that support not just themselves and their biological families but also, critically, their faith families and potentially the nation and the world as well! **Faith Resources are not just born-again Christian men and women, they are successful parent-leaders!**

Therefore, in this context, the substance of faith is the full realisation of the God in whom you have chosen to believe, the substance of faith is to cease from all forms of godliness that deny the power thereof, the substance of faith is the emergence of a new breed of Christians who truly understand and live the Word of God by the power of His Spirit, the substance of faith is to achieve not just giant strides of destiny but to understand that "every creation contains an invisible command from God to multiply and become more"[47] and thus really arrive at the ultimate destination and to hear the Master say, "well done!"[48]

Section Overview:

There then appears to be three levels of faith: (1) Faith in **God** - through Jesus Christ, (2) Faith, by God's grace, in **self** and (3) Faith, by the very same God's grace, in **others**. Faith in God essentially entails the ability to believe the impossible and the willingness to believe God and trust in God as well as in his actions and promises. Faith in self and others also entails complete confidence, belief or trust in a person or "thing" which essentially requires allegiance, loyalty etc. So to be faithful is to have faith and remaining true, constant and loyal; to be consistently reliable, truthful and steadfast – whether you are "leading" or "following". Faith requires these three dimensions in order to be true,

---

[47] Mike Murdock, 'One-Minute Pocket Bible P.18
[48] Matthew 25:21,23

whole and complete! Little wonder Scripture admonishes: "*...Believe IN the LORD your God so shall ye be established; believe his prophets, so shall ye prosper.*"[49] Therefore, faith in God that lacks faith in self and in others is worthless because it can't produce action - as you'll be so "spiritual" that you are no earthly good!

Our faith really has no substance and has no real meaning outside the context of the superstructure of "receive" and "prove" - understanding biblical truth and its real-life day-to-day application. Therefore, the substance of faith is not just the emergence of a breed of people called Christians, but Christians who are actually Faith Resources! People that will boldly exercise and demonstrate such "three-dimensional" faith which dispels all fears – apart from the fear of God! People that will dare to take all necessary, positive and godly actions that unlock the "creative-empowerment" in them, which enables them to both "be" and "become" all that God had called them to be and become! People that will help restore the family, corporate nature and organic concept of church rather than promote individualism or merely pursue organizational and structural drives. Such is the experiential nature of this "three-dimensional-faith" – the joy of fellowship and hearts strangely warmed. Wherefore, God is truly encountered and experienced and lives changed: faith is not simply a matter of correct belief and sound theology alone, but also of evidently and unquestionably changed and impacted lives vis-à-vis the lives of our faith children and their realised callings and strides of destiny!

---

[49] 2 Chronicles 20:20c (KJV)

This is the new creation where there is no room for distinctions in the family systems, a new creation in which all distinctions (i.e. biological vs. faith relationships) vanish. This new creation is without distinction of person. This, my friends, is the new breed![50]

---

[50] See 2 Corinthians 5:17 & Colossians 3:11 (AMP) as well as Galatians 6:15 (NASS & AMP)

Faith Metaphors
The Seeds and Fruit of Faith

SEEDS = ATTITUDES = CHARACTER

*N*ow *it is important to* note that in this context, I have taken resources to mean exactly the same as "seeds" and that these seeds are gifts that emanate directly from the very image of God. The summation of the combinations of seeds that we carry inside us, determine our attitudes to life and the summation of our attitudes determines our personality and ultimate character.

We have often heard it said that our attitude determines our altitude in life, and I believe this to be true and there is even mathematical proof to back this up.

Exercise: *The aim of this exercise is to find that one thing in life which really equates to a 100% and thus could be deemed the most important. Start by listing out all the things that are important to you in life: God? Family? Money? Success? Power? etc. Then equating each letter of the alphabet (A-Z) to the numbers 1-26; sum up each item on your lists and you will sadly discover that none gives 100%! Only attitude! So none of the things you think are important (not even God, I dare say) can determine your altitude in life only your attitude towards those things on your list. Selah....*

Men do not decide their future. They decide their habits and attitudes and these in turn, by the divine laws of nature, decide their future. But whilst our attitude may truly determine our altitude and indeed "the seasons (we)[52] enter", our character ultimately determines whether or not we remain at those altitudes. So, indeed your attitude may determine your altitude for it is the only thing that sums up to 100%; Character sums up to 77% and 7 stands for perfection. Therefore, though it may be true (arguably) that there is no such thing as a perfect leader or parent – for I know at least one: God – your attitude may take you to the top but only your character can keep you perfectly in your place, if it's godly, because no one else will "fit"!

The Word of God is the only true seed[53] that forms our attitude and character as good fruit, that will ensure maximum altitude (prosperity) and 'good success'[54] - both here and after.

The Word of God is CHRIST Himself (John 1:1-5) and Christ in us - our hope of glory - is the image of God that we bear/carry inside us and reflect through the Holy Spirit that indwells us (Romans 8:29, Colossians 1:15, 1 Corinthians 15:49, 2 Corinthians 3:18). This same Christ in us; is the fullness of God (Ephesians 3 particularly vv. 14-21). As leaders, therefore, *we are to be noble workmen that will get God's approval as true Faith Resources (Acts 17:11 and 2 Timothy 2:15). Why? How? Because we truly live the Word by the Power of His Spirit such that our lives, words and actions become more of a sermon than those we preach and teach.*

---

[52] Mike Murdock, 'One-Minute Pocket Bible', P.22
[53] See Luke 8:11
[54] See Joshua 1:8 (KJV)

Are You a Noble Seed?
(What Does It Mean To Be Noble?!)

O ne of the noblest pursuits any human can have is to totally submit to and seek God and then, as a child of God, to embark upon getting to know and understand Him better. A process that theologians might classify as *"faith seeking understanding* – wherefore we believe not necessarily because we understand, but we understand because we believe![55]

The best way we can accomplish this is to look carefully at the book God has written, the Bible, which communicates who He is and His plan for you and I (mankind)[56]. The Bible spots and commends the Berean Christians in this regard (Acts 17:11).

When the Bible assures that the effective, fervent prayers of the righteous avail much[57] (i.e. always answered?! Wow!), I am of the opinion that these are prayers based on the Word of God. The Bible also assures that even when we do not know what to pray about that the Spirit of God will search our hearts and make intercessions on our behalf[58]. I am convinced that the Holy Spirit will intercede for us using the Word of God as seen in Jude 9 (AMP).

---

[55] Stanley J. Grenz & Roger E. Olson, *'Who Needs Theology? An Invitation to the Study of God'* (Leicester, England: InterVarsity Press, 1996)
[56] Jim George, 'The Bare Bones Bible Handbook' (Oregon: Harvest House Publishers, 2006), 303
[57] James 5:16 (KJV)
[58] Romans 8:26 (KJV)

Therefore when the Spirit comes to intercede for you and searches your heart, will He find the Word hidden therein?[59]

> Q: *The crucial question at this juncture is: how regularly and when last did you study and hide the word of God in your heart – even according to Psalm 119:11?*

To keep your main resource reservoir (i.e. your spiritual tank) full, you must be faithful in your study of God's word, sustain your prayer life and maintain your integrity. That is the only way that you can take hold of and live out the essential seeds that every true Faith Resource is made of.

Galatians 5:22 lists some of these all-important seeds[60] that we carry inside us: seeds that we must allow yield the fruit of goodly and Godly attitude and character in us, if we truly carry the image of God - *love, joy, peace, long-suffering, gentleness (mild or kindly character/nature), goodness, faith, meekness (humble, patient, longsuffering, submissive) and temperance (restraint/moderation).*

---

[59] See Psalm 119:11

[60] Note that I have used seeds and fruits interchangeably because a fruit is only but the seed inside it. The seed determines the fruit!

Q: What are these seeds to be used for? Just how many of these seeds show forth as tangible fruit in your life, attitudes and disposition to people?

Some of the important attitudes that these seeds will produce in us include *humility* and *honesty*. 'Jesus speaks about the attitudes and actions that should characterise (our) daily life – *forgiveness, faithfulness, thankfulness and commitment,*'[61] just to mention a few.

Q: Just How committed are you to your God-given relationships?

A person's character is the combination of traits (attitude as determined by our seeds) and qualities distinguishing the individual nature of that person: a moral force - *integrity*, reputation, capacity, position and status. To write, print, inscribe or engrave it is the person's mark upon the sands of time. It is the person's *distinguishing mark* [62] (his/her *life's "signature"*!).

---

[61] Jim George, 193
[62] Collins Dictionary, 258-259

There are two types of wisdom: earthly and heavenly (Proverbs 3[63] – especially from verse 13ff - describes the nature and content of this divine wisdom). As far as I am concerned, one of the most important distinguishing marks that should characterise any true Faith Resource is heavenly *wisdom*[64]. Wisdom is the ability or result of an ability to think and act, utilising *knowledge,* experience, *understanding, common sense* (that is not so common) and insight.[65]

I always thought that knowledge brings understanding but I was stunned to see that understanding brings knowledge, for God gives knowledge to the understanding (see Proverbs 2).

It is worthy of note that the fear of God is indeed the beginning of wisdom (Proverbs 9:10, Psalm 111:10 and Job 28:28) and the counsel that wisdom is *"profitable"* to direct (Ecclesiastics 10:10) would strongly indicate that wisdom is a principal tool for ultimate success (including *"wealth"* creation, distribution and sustenance). Hence we are told: with wisdom we not only build and establish, we also fill our chambers with all precious and pleasant riches![66] Now

---

[63] See both NIV & MSG translations

[64] Wisdom in itself is a hugely complex discourse perhaps due to a lack of clear definition of the term and 'the difficult nature of the poetic language within which most of the wisdom material has been found.' (Homan, 1674). We could easily spend unimaginable lengths of time on it, but we cannot afford to digress too much at this point.

[65] Collins Dictionary, 1714.

[66] See Proverbs 24

it is crucially important to note that God Himself has **characterised** Himself with wisdom, thus making wisdom an 'attribute of God'. Wisdom characterises us with such virtues as **industry**, honesty, sobriety – to refrain from excess, chastity, concern for good reputation and includes **technical skill** (Exodus 28:3), **military prowess** (Isaiah 10:13), **shrewdness** (including **political shrewdness** and **leadership skills** etc.) (I Kings 2:6). We can be wisdom personified for wisdom is a person and bears children[67] and because 'Jesus is wisdom'.[68]

I make a bold attempt to construct a working definition: **wisdom is God's own character; an ultimate gift from God[69] through Jesus Christ and begins with our faith in Him as Lord and Saviour; enabling us to grasp the essence of life and also an art-form that equips us with the learned skill of how to succeed in life.[70]**

In concluding this section, I humbly submit that to be a noble seed is to prioritise the Word and conform to the very image of God: wisdom personified. Curiously though, scriptures admonish that we learn from nature, especially even smaller creatures!

---

[67] see Mathew 11:19b (KJV)

[68] Zondervan Compact Bible Dictionary, (Michigan: Zondervan, 1993), 606 (See also: Proverbs 3:19)

[69] For it is He that gives bread to the eater and seeds to the sower, the One in whom we live, move and have our being and in whom all things consist.

[70] Holman, 1675

Lessons From Nature
(What have insects and rodents got to do with it?)

There are four small creatures, wisest of the wise. They include **ants.** Frail as they are, they get plenty of food in for the winter.

There are also **marmots** – a kind of rodent. Vulnerable as they are, they manage to arrange rock-solid homes for themselves.

Thirdly, locusts – leaderless insects, yet they strip the field like an army regiment.

Finally, lizards – easy to catch, but they sneak past vigilant palace guards[71].

---

[71] Eugene H. Peterson, The Book of Proverbs – The Message, (Colorado: NAVPRESS, 2004), 103.

But What's Up With The Ants!

Could the amazing fact that some of these insects and bugs 'can lift 850 times their own weight'[72] be due to their shear strength, tactics and skill or could it be practical wisdom or could there be a deeper reason for such profound abilities and success?

The fact that God Himself directs us to the ants for much needed wisdom (Proverbs 6:6) ought to command a closer attention to this "tiny" yet curious and significant creature. Here are just a very few amazing facts:

✓ *The total weight of all the ants in the world is the same as, if not larger than, that of all humans.*
✓ *Some ants (and other bugs) can support up to 100 times and even 850 times their own (body) weight.*
✓ The largest ant colony ever found was over 6,000km or 3,750 miles wide.
✓ Ants are the longest living of all insects, living up to 30 years.
✓ One ant species holds the record for the fastest movement within the animal kingdom, proportional to its size. (*We are told that if a man could run as fast for his size, as an ant, he could run as fast as a racehorse!*).
✓ The ant is one of the world's strongest creatures in relation to its size.
✓ *Dozens of colonies of the world's smallest ant (of the over 12,000 known different species) could live in the brain case of the world's largest ant.*

---

[72] Brenda Clarke et al 'Weird and Wonderful Animals' Tick Tock Entertainment Ltd (Tunbridge, Kent: Tick Tock Entertainment Ltd, 2010), 20.

✓ Ants move an estimated 50 tons of soil per year in one square mile (farming).

✓ Fire ants cause an estimated $5 billion worth of damage in North America per year.

✓ Ants and humans are the only creatures that farm other creatures. They are farmers! They sometimes herd or tend to insects of other species.

✓ *Ants have two stomachs, one to hold food for themselves, and one for (food to be shared by) others.*

✓ Ants can be found on every continent except ANTarctica.

✓ *Some ants can swim and most ants can survive around 24 hours underwater.*

✓ Ants have two eyes, each made up of many smaller eyes called compound eyes, although some ants have no eyes.

✓ Some birds put ants in their feathers because ants squirt formic acid which gets rid of the parasites.

✓ Certain ant species defend (farm) plants in exchange for food and shelter.

✓ Some worker ants are given the job of taking the rubbish from the nest and putting it outside in a special rubbish dump! *If a worker ant has found a good source of food, it leaves a trail of scent so that the other ants in the colony can find the food.*

✓ *Ants' worst enemies are not us, but other ants.*[73]

So if "mere" ants can accomplish these phenomenal feats and much more, why do we, comparatively, seem to be underachieving as humans, especially as Christians?

---

[73] www.antark.net/ant-facts/#.UfFKtNKTj6Q;
www.lingolex.com/ants.html;
www.insects.about.com/od/antsbeeswasps/a/10-cool-facts-about-ants.htm

Even on a corporate level such as the Church! Might we be better placed as a whole if we (at least) put our needless self-indulgences, un-progressive, uncharitable, unprofitable and unhelpful diversions/distractions/amusements/debates etc. that are neither edifying to us nor glorying to God. What about our "denominational"[75] lines? Jesus's example per His encounter with the Samaritan woman (John 4:1-42) shows our model (Jesus Christ) crossing such unhelpful boundaries as culture, class (religious & social), tribal and even "ethical" boundaries. Can we learn from our Master's example?

Of all the very many amazing facts about ants, I have only stated a handful and even so there are three of these that strike me the most: the fact that ants, like humans, are their own worst enemies! But they, unlike humans, have learnt to set this aside by allowing other, smaller (perhaps weaker) ants to live in their brain case and the fact that they feed themselves with one stomach and collect food for other ants with the second – "psychic income"!

I agree with Matthew Henry's extoling in this matter: The ants help one another: if one has a grain of corn too big for her to carry home, her neighbours will come to her assistance. **"How long wilt thou waste thy time? How long wilt thou love thy ease, and when will thou learn**

---

[75] Now whilst I believe that this hydra-headed monster of religiousity - denominationalism – can be very unhelpful and damaging to Kingdom mind-set; I am by no means suggesting that dogmatic lines should be compromised, let alone laid aside! However flimsy lines (e.g. baptism in the name of the Father, Son & Holy Spirit v Baptism in the name of Jesus) ought to be erased if any progress is to be made in fulfilling our purposes & destinies as Faith Resources. For these are at best systematic theological constructs and at worst mere opinions.

to deny thyself, and to take pains? How long wilt thou delay, and put off, and trifle away thy opportunities? And when wilt thou stir up thyself to do what thou hast to do, which if it be not done, will leave thee ever undone?" The ant has no guides and rulers but simply follows the instinct of nature. We have the Holy Spirit who is our nature's instinct! Moreover, we have the bonus of parents, masters, ministers, magistrates etc, to also help put us in mind of our duty, to direct us in it. We should thus be roused and indeed excel in the duties of our particular calling as Faith Resources![76]

The "V" Formation

In the same vein, John Maxwell skillfully draws from the intriguing nature of geese: Why do geese fly along in a "V" formation?

Because they support each other - riding on each other's thrusts - and thus the whole flock adds at least 71 percent greater flying range than if each bird flew on its own. Whenever a goose falls out of formation, it suddenly feels the drag and resistance of trying to go it alone and quickly

---

[76] Matthew Henry's Commentary, P.743

gets back into formation to take advantage of the lifting power of the bird immediately in front, each honking to encourage the one ahead to keep up its speed and when the lead goose gets tired, he rotates back into the "V" and another goose flies the point. When a goose gets sick or is wounded by gunfire and falls out, two other geese fall out of formation and follow it down to help and protect it. They stay with the goose until it is either able to fly again or dead, and then they launch out on their own or with another formation to catch up with their group.

Q: What do we as humans say to or about each other when we honk from behind?

Whoever was the first to call another person a "silly goose" didn't know enough about geese! If we, as the people of God have as much sense as the goose, ants etc. we will stay in formation, taking turns in doing hard jobs and stand with each other like that, travel on one another's thrust and thus advancing God's Kingdom more quickly and easily. That is wisdom![77]

As humans (especially as Christians) we seem to be seriously underachieving in light of these amazing facts. These tiny creatures seem to have successfully overcome

---

[77] John Maxwell, 'Developing The Leaders Around You', P.8 *We are told that as each bird in the V flaps its wings, it creates an UPLIFT for the bird immediately behind it!*

the selfish and self-centered spirit of "individualism" that has so destroyed our Christian witness. Indeed, we need to learn wisdom from the ants, the geese and nature at large if we must understand what it means to be Faith Resources and function as such. This is the only way forward for us as Christians if we really desire to see God's will and Kingdom here on earth.

The Cockroach Phenomenon

The essence of this critical and crucial character requirement (wisdom) was one of the early lessons that my spiritual/faith father (Apostle Abam) taught me through what I have since come to term the Cockroach Phenomenon or Pressure-Stress-Test Theory.

He said to me, "Son, if you stepped on a cockroach and squashed it, would blood come out of it?"

I considered this question in my heart. The above image conjured up in my mind as I intently thought about what seemed to me at the time like a trick question. And then I answered in a rather unsure manner, "No, daddy."

My father then proceeded to ask, "Why?" This threw me somewhat off-balance as, again, I intently thought upon this follow-up question whilst bringing to bear all of my many experiences and encounters with cockroaches whilst growing up in Nigeria! And then as if inspired, I sheepishly answered almost rhetorically, "Because they have no blood?" Then with a sense of strange relief I heard him say, "That's right! What comes out is filth and dirt because that's all they have inside of them; not blood!" And in this same way you must ensure that no matter what anybody does to you and no matter the pressures that you come under, no dirt or filth should ever come out of you because that's not in you; only the blood of Jesus in which there is no trace of evil!

I believe that David, being a very wise man, also probably knew this as well. In the midst of his crazy conflict with his father (King Saul), Gene Edwards vividly depicts his state of mind, "Better he kill me than I learn his ways. Better he kill me than I become as he is. I shall not practice the ways that cause kings to go mad. I will not throw spears, nor will I allow hatred to grow in my heart. I will not avenge. I will not destroy the Lord's anointed. Not now. Not ever!"[78]

This cockroach phenomenon, as well as David's example aptly expresses the ageless truth that, "There is a vast difference between the outward clothing of the Spirit's power and the inward filling of the Spirit's life. In the first, despite the power, the hidden man of the heart may remain unchanged. In the latter, that monster is dealt with."[79]

---

[78] Gene Edwards, 'A Tale of Three Kings – *A Study in Brokenness*', (Newman, Georgia: Seedsowers, 1992), 36-37
[79] Gene Edwards, 41

That for me was one of the most valuable lessons ever learnt in my strides of destiny as a true Faith Resource and the positive dimension of this cockroach phenomenon is one that will ever remain in the fore of my mind. This conviction to allow not just the Spirit's power but (crucially) also, the Spirit's life to flow through me, is one vital element that has continually helped me through critical conflict and cross-road points in my life.

Now What Must I Do?
(Reasonable Expectations)

"Commitment is your final decision to meet the needs of the ones God has called you to serve."[83] Faith Resources are ordinary Christian people (like you and I!) in whom the seven-fold Holy Spirit of God dwells, thus enabling them to exude wisdom, understanding, counsel, might/power, knowledge and the fear of God.[84] These attributes enable us to commit to firm and definite action with neither hesitation nor delay.

The out-living consequences of this attribute are simply inexhaustible, but the following list only simply sets the general frame of reference for who and what Faith Resources are and what they do or what can be expected of/from them at any given time.

➤ Faith Resources, being living evidential proof and "substance" of faith - like Abraham in Genesis 12 - not only understand that God's word leads to faith (Gen 12:1-3) , which in turn leads to obedience (Gen 12:4-6) and then blessing (Gen 12:7-9) but that testing is a critical part of the package of this highly sought-after blessing (Gen 12:10-20).

➤ Faith Resources live by faith and thus make decisions on the basis of the Word of God (Rom 10:17) and seek to glorify God alone (Rom 4:19-20). True Faith Resources are not in a hurry, but willing to "wait" (Isa 28:16, Heb 6:12). We obey God in spite of circumstances or

---

[83] Mike Murdock, 28
[84] See: Revelation 1:4, 3:1, 4:5 and 5:6 and Isaiah 11:2 (AMP)

consequences, and we are not afraid of what others may say or do (Heb 11:29-30).

Q: Are you living by faith?

➢ As men (and women of course!), if we have true faith and belief in God, know Jesus as our personal Lord and Saviour and are truly filled with the Holy Spirit (not just the outward clothing of the Spirit's Power but most importantly, the inward filling of the Spirit's life), then we are filled with all *fullness of God* (Ephesians 3:19). The Greek root of the word fullness is *pleroma (play-row-mah)* and it describes a ship with a full cargo and crew and a town with no empty houses. *Pleroma* strongly describes fullness and completion, abundance, extensive in quantity (and quality!) etc. Therefore, we are able to do all things through Christ who strengthens us (Philippians 4:13). Indeed, even exceedingly and abundantly above all expectations, thoughts and imaginations of men! (Ephesians 3:20)

Q: Is it possible that faith most likely always has an element of risk?!

➤ Faith opens the door for us to be filled with all the fullness of God. When this happens, we enter a higher dimension of living, wherefore, not only do we demonstrate the outward clothing of the Spirit's power, but, crucially too, the inward filling of the Spirit's life. Not that we become so spiritual or heavenly-minded that we are no earthly good, but our feet are firmly planted on the ground and we deal maturely with reality whilst allowing Christ to live through us at greater dimensions whereby our true (spiritual) person shines forth!

➤ God knows we need to be sufficient in all things and has made us *RESOURCEFUL!* The enemy will try to deny us the reality of this blessing because he knows that our personal "problems" might hinder and distract others from coming to faith. However, we must bear in mind that the wicked may try to out-manoeuvre God, but God will have His way (Proverbs 19:21; 21:30).

➤ No matter what "resources" we may lean on, only God gives success (Proverbs 21:31). We may be permitted to use what we have and whatever means God provides (remember that God asked Moses,: "What is in your hand?"), but we must put our faith in God alone.[85]

➤ God has not only put us together, but has also bestowed us with all the "seeds" we require to have "good" success, but the questions are: Are you a part of God's plan? Are you playing your part? Are you helping Him? Note that I am by no means alluding to the secular idea that "Heaven helps those who help themselves". Although there may be some truth elements in there, but please DO NOT

---

[85] Warren W. Wierse, 'Nelson's Quick Reference Commentary', (Nashville: Thomas Nelson, 1991), 426

"help" yourself, because the truth is that you cannot! However, God expects you to co-operate and partner with Him according to His divine plan and purpose(s) for your life, and indeed by realising your true nature as a "FAITH RESOURCE"!

➤ Faith Resources are leaders. Being a good leader involves reproducing yourself in others, knowing that leaders are parents of sorts. Every parent believes that one day that son or daughter will become somebody great. Therefore, Faith Resources never give up on the people they are investing in – their children! Faith Resources reproduce themselves by being parents, teachers, friends etc. - exposing their children to the challenges of ministry and actually sending them into ministry[86]

Q: *"Who will take your place? There is no success without a successor." (Selah)*[87]

➤ Faith Resources understand that **leading leaders lead leaders** and that it takes a leader to attract a leader, know a leader, grow a leader and show a leader. They therefore know how to develop the leaders around them and how to help others reach their full potential and

---

[86] Dag Heward-Mills 'The Art of Leadership' (England: Parchment House, 2003), 267, 286-288
[87] Peter Drucker quoted by John C. Maxwell in: Developing The Leaders Around You, P. 10

accomplish their destiny.[88] Their greatest joy is to coach a dream team of leaders who will in turn reproduce generations of leaders (a faith family!). As parent-leaders, Faith Resources become excellent in engaging this lifelong commitment, not just with bowels of mercy, but crucially also with great expressions of their love to and for their faith children through **words of affirmation, quality time, gifts (not just receiving, but giving as well!), acts of service and of course staying physically in touch.**[89]

➤ Faith Resources are merciful and giving. They are exemplary leaders who function effectively as experts, cheerleaders, lovers and referees.[90] Faith Resources, ultimately, are "good" people and thus do not hesitate to use themselves as examples. They therefore receive God's blessings and divine ordering because they are good people/leaders who leave an inheritance for all those in their spheres of influence.

➤ Faith Resources are successful people, not just because of what they possess/have, contain/carry, achieve etc., but ultimately because of how much fruit they bear i.e. spiritual fruit e.g. children, converts, mentees, successors, successful trainees etc. Those that they have actually taught to catch fish as well as set up to shine! (see Luke 8:16). They are incredible benefactors with bowels of mercy! Therefore, they are channels of blessings and are trees

---

[88] John C. Maxwell, 'Developing the Leaders Around You', (Nashville, Tennessee: Thomas Nelson, 1995)

[89] Gary Chapman, 'The Heart of The Five Love Languages', (Chicago: Northfield Publishing, 2007) – Edited by Tracey D. Lawrence

[90] Jim George, 299-307

planted by the rivers of living waters i.e. Christ (Psalm 1). *Whatever* Faith Resources do *prospers.*

Q: *We all know that God desires mercy and NOT sacrifice: But what is the difference between mercy and sacrifice?*

Now I think the major difference is the POINT OF ACTION. Sacrifice is one touch beyond the point of mercy. I believe that Scripture also marks this distinction when we are charged, 'Never walk away from someone who deserves help, your hand is God's for that person. Don't tell your neighbour, "Maybe some other time," or "Try me tomorrow," when the money's right there in your pocket.'[91] Sacrifice is a *"religious act"*, mercy is an *attitude and* entails pardon to an offender, and that's why God requires us to leave our gifts at the altar, compassion to the poor, weak, sick etc. (the needy generally). Mercy is one of the cardinal virtues/character of a true FAITH RESOURCE (see James 2:1-13) and is one of the vital elemental seeds that the fruit of the Spirit consists (see Gal. 5:22-23). Mercy is like money. Your deposits determine your withdrawal (see Matthew 5:7 and 6:15).

---

[91] Proverbs 3:27-28 (MSG)

Q: What then is sacrificial mercy?

➤ Faith Resources are, in fact, rivers with a never drying source (God), for they are a perfect image and inscription of God. They are rivers and not lakes. They have no *"backdoor fear"* and thus not afraid to help and support people to become as (and even much more) successful as/than they are. It is instructive to note the interesting difference between rivers and lakes:

RIVERS	LAKES
A body of water that runs continuously	A body of water that lies still
Where "water" is *spent*	Where water is *stored*[92]
A river (for the most part) is naturally composed	A lake is (more often than not) typically man-made

Q: Do you know what a lake can become if enough "sediment" (i.e. jealousy, selfishness, meanness, grudges, unforgiveness, etc.) build up inside of it? A swamp! (See Ezekiel 47:11 and be warned)

---

[92] Therefore you ought to take heed if your mentality is, "Get all you can and can all you get"!

To be a swamp is to be overburdened or overwhelmed by *excess* or a great number of "foreign" elements, causing the "ship" or "boat" to sink or fill with "water" and submerge! (Compare with Pleroma)[93]

> Faith Resources do not just have spiritual children; they also have spiritual parents. In fact, Faith Resources consciously and deliberately establish a foundation of spiritual faith family systems and operate and hold themselves accountable to this systemic structure. The solidly structured parent-child mechanism within this system ensures adequate and healthy two-way oversight and care, just as you would expect to find in a normal biological family where grooming exists. These foundations are critical as they encourage the average Christian to take up their priesthood and emerge as a truly new breed (i.e. Faith Resources)[94]. In this sort of environment, encouragement, as companions, at times of tiredness and even positive or constructive "discouragement", engenders bigger dreams than might otherwise be dreamt, help to hear God more clearly and turn prayers into action![95]

> We are told of the missional trend of the re-emerging Church: Baby boomers who are now seeking to reconnect with the Church because faith seeds were sown in them. Someone took time, effort and perhaps even pain to set them a frame of reference and nurtured them on their faith journey. Those who did that for the boomers are indeed Faith Resources.[96]

---

[93] Milan Ford, *83 Things I Wish The Black Church Would Stop Doing,* (USA: The PewView.Com, 2009), 26-29.

[94] (2 Corinthians 5:17)

[95] Rebekah Brettle with Lyndhall Bywater, 'Neighbours, Transform Your Street!' (Lancaster: Sovereign World, 2012), 98.

[96] Roger Standing, 'Re-emerging Church – Strategies for Reaching a Returning Generation' (UK: BRF- Bible Reading Fellowship, 2008).

*Do you have spiritual parents and oversight? Who are they? How accessible are they to you as well as to your faith children? Do you have access to their parents? Does everyone in this family system have as well as know and understand their own **recourse protocols** to relevant and appropriate levels of parental authorities? Did you know that in order to be in effective authority, you must be under authority? The centurion understood this and Jesus counted and acknowledged this as great faith. (Matthew 8:13). So just how great is your faith o ye Faith Resources?*

➤ To obtain the fullness of God requires one key attitude: *PATIENCE* (James 1:4). Ever heard of the saying, 'Good things come to those who wait'? I saw this in play when during one of our family times – playing monopoly – our youngest daughter read a book as we played and hassled to accumulate and "prosper"! She even got one of us to help roll the dice on her go, not paying much attention to the hassles required of the game, yet she prospered in the monopoly world more than we did! I think that real life can be much the same if we imbibe godly patience as admonished by scriptures.

➤ Faith Resources have a default position in all circumstances to "start by doing what is necessary, then what is possible, and suddenly you are doing the impossible"[97]. In other words, once you begin to do the

---

[97] St. Francis of Assisi, goodreads.com (Accessed Tuesday 14/10/13)

necessary, you find yourself in the realms of possibilities and suddenly you find yourself doing the impossible, because in the realms of possibilities, nothing is impossible! Therefore, Faith Resources are men (and women!) who operate at those realms where they are able to do the seemingly impossible, even effortlessly. Why? Because they are dedicated to ensuring that they actually do whatever is *"necessary"* to fulfill God's purposes not just for themselves but also for the realisation of destinies for all those in their spheres of influence (See: Luke 1:37, Genesis 18:14, Jeremiah 32:17, Ephesians 3:20 and Philippians 4:13).

➢ Faith Resources are very *humble* people. 'I used to think that God's gifts were on shelves one above the other, and that the taller we grew in Christian character the more easily we could reach them. I now find that God's gifts are on shelves one beneath the other and that it is not a question of growing taller but of stooping lower.'[98] Faith Resources are able to obtain the best of God's gifts, riches and glory because they understand that 'humility (as an important *attitude*) is the source of all true greatness'[99], but they also have the requisite *character* to sustain those blessings and remain at the top! It is important to note that it is only the STRONG that can be humble – for it takes bold *courage* to be humble! Little wonder Scripture encourages us to be strong and courageous! With this godly courage should come divine wisdom (common sense that is not so common!); for though it takes courage to hunt on the back of a lion, it takes common sense to know when to "run". Faith Resources know to run under the shadow of the Almighty and remain there! They have divine courage to effect change and strength in God for the things they

---

[98] F.B. Meyer
[99] Fenelon, Nelson's Quick Reference, 276

cannot change by human strength but, crucially, also, "the wisdom to know the difference".[100]

➤ Faith Resources *do things for God* and *God does things for them.* However, they understand that although faith is a precious gift, it is not a luxury, but a necessity; it is also for "common" people and not just for "great" leaders. We need faith for worshipping (Hebrews 11:4), as well as for working (v 7), walking (vv 8-9) and warring (vv 30-34). In any area of life where you ignore faith, you will sin (Romans 14:23). Faith Resources know too well that you can live by faith and still appear to be defeated and that not everybody who trusted God was "delivered" or "protected" (vv 36-40). **But the important thing is not God's** ***deliverance***[101]**; it is God's *approval*** (v 39). Faith Resources master the ability to *endure* when others are *giving up*.[102] *Bear in mind that deliverance can mean different things to different people. 'We cry too often to be delivered from the punishment, instead of the sin that lies behind it. We are anxious to escape from the things that cause us pain rather than the things that cause God pain'.* Our concept of deliverance is often very warped, but we can learn from the attitude and example of Shedrach, Meshach and Abednigo in Daniel 3.

➤ Faith Resources understand the process of time and the challenges they must overcome. They also know this process: *God's word leads to faith (Romans 10:17), faith leads to obedience (Hebrews 11:8), Obedience leads to blessing, blessing leads to testing and testing leads to testimonies!* They understand that patience is the weapon that forces deception to reveal itself and thus fully embrace James 1:4, but crucially have

---

[100] St. Frances of Assisi, goodreads.com (Accessed Tuesday 14/10/13)
[101] G Campbell Morgan, in Nelson's Quick Ref., 822
[102] Nelson's, 820

mastered the art of *patient persistence!* They understand that when you live by faith, you make your decisions on the basis of the Word of God and you seek to glorify God alone (Romans 4:19-20). They understand that true faith is not in a hurry; it is willing to trustingly and patiently wait[103] and this waiting is not characterised by *"idleness/inaction/doing nothing"*. Faith Resources obey God in spite of circumstances or consequences and are not afraid of what others may say or do (see Hebrews 11:29-30).

> *Did you know: it's the seed which grows, the yeast which spreads, the mustard seed which skyrockets, and the net which draws the fish? All the workers (Faith Resources) need to do is sow, throw, mix and…wait. That is the enduring patience required of Parent-Leaders by their faith children. It's both easy and incredibly-terribly difficult (all at once!). Will you support and patiently wait for your faith children to grow and skyrocket?*

➢ Faith Resources understand that false accusations may often be the last stage before their supernatural promotion. They are thus tried and tested people. **Because they are intrinsically good, no amount of testing, crushing pressure, trial or tribulation can cause them to give off bad, whether in attitude, behaviour, character etc.!** They understand that blessing leads to

---

[103] Isaiah 28:16 (KJV & MSG); Hebrews 6:12

testing and these tests are for three main reasons: to prove whether our faith is real; to help our faith grow; and to *bring glory to the Lord* (1 Peter 1:6-9; James 1:1-8)[104]. *You can indeed 'judge the quality of their faith from the way they behave'[105], even under pressure, tests and stress!* They are indeed *apostles, even in the market place.*

➤ Faith Resources are true noble seeds and understand the positive dimensions of the Cockroach Phenomenon; in that these Christians remain kings and priests regardless. Just as David remained David as noted by Gene Edwards in his book: 'A Tale of Three Kings'.[106]

➤ Faith Resources have been taught to say who they are. Note that Jesus spoke of Himself confidently. He said He was the way, the truth and the life. He said He was the door. He said He was the good shepherd etc... Declare yourself; for it's important for people to know who you are.

➤ Faith Resources are those that determine that "whatever it takes" - that sermon in their spirit must be preached, that exploit and inspiration from God must be fulfilled, that book in their hearts must be written, that story shared, that idea born, that film recorded etc. A Faith Resource is the one who conceived the idea and bore the system for keeping that "old rusty well" going and his/her protégés are all those who kept the legacy of that system.

---

[104] Nelson's Quick Reference, 22-23
[105] Tertullian, Ditto, 821
[106] Gene Edwards, 'A Tale of Three Kings – A Study In Brokenness' (Wheaton Illinois: Tyndale House Publishers, 1992).

The story has been told of this old rusty well in the desert with a bottle of water and a note. Sojourners are required by this note to "waste" the bottle of water to prime the well; drink all they want fill back the bottle and bury it with the note for the next sojourner – once they've drank to their heart's content! What would you do?!

➤ Faith Resources are constantly on guard because we never know when God is using the everyday things of life to test our faith. Note that the men in Gideon's army were tested by the way they drank water (Judges 7). Lot was tested by a disagreement over land (Gen. 13:6ff). Israel was tested by thirst (Exodus 15:22-27) and Moses was tested by the complaining of the people (Num. 20:1-13).[108]

➤ Faith Resources are truly wise people in that they will hear the Word of God (Prov. 1:5) and obey it (Prov. 12:15), store up what is learned (Prov. 9:9, 10:14), win the lost (Prov. 11:30), turn from sin (Prov. 14:16), control the tongue (Prov. 10:19, 16:23) and be diligent (Prov. 10:5). These wise people will inherit glory (Prov. 3:35), bring joy to others (Prov. 10:1, 15:20), have his or her needs met (Prov. 21:20) and have strength for war (Prov. 24:5-6).[109]

➤ Faith Resources are action people. They are righteous in that they are merciful and generous and wise even in winning souls (see Proverbs 11:30). They "put their

---

[108] Warren W. Wiersbe, 147
[109] Warren W. Wiersbe, Nelson Quick Reference, p.412

money to work for His Kingdom, work hard, live simply and give generously so that they can help the needy and promote the gospel message around the world", starting right where they are - their immediate spheres of influence![110] If we understand that every 10 minutes about 210 people die of hunger and almost a thousand people die and go to hell then, as followers of Christ, we will take these matters seriously and take our places as FAITH RESOURCES!

➤ Finally, but by no means the end of my list, Faith Resources are great visionaries who understand that it takes a leader with vision to see the future leader within a person. They are great and indeed "GOOD" leaders who understand that *leading leaders lead leaders.* They take time not only to understand the **desires** of those they lead but actively harness those desires with great mastery and sensitivity. You become a leading leader by taking your place as a Faith Resource as ONLY then will you understand that those "under" you, whom you lead, are also leaders themselves and begin to lead those leaders to become the leaders that God had called and ordained them to be! Christian Wogu comments that good leaders pay their debts and I believe that part of that debt is to build successive leaders! For "there is no success without a successor."[111]

Critical Note:

"As much as potential leaders (your successors) respect (your) knowledge and ability, these are secondary matters to them. They

---

[110] Phil Moore, "Matthew" p.70
[111] John Maxwell, 'Developing The Leaders Around You – *How To Help Others Reach Their Full Potential',* (Thomas Nelson: Nashville, 1995), 11.

*don't care how much (you) know until they know how much (you)
care about their needs, their dreams and their desires."*

Once a parent-leader proves to really believe in his
children's ability and that he is genuinely interested in their
well-being, they become activated in a remarkable way and
gain the required momentum that propels them on giant
strides of destiny.[112] Indeed, your lasting value is measured
by succession. I believe that this fact largely underpins the
irrefutable "LAW OF LEGACY" and will determine what
people *genuinely* say at your funeral!

Q: *What is success to you? Can you reconcile
your answer with what God is doing in your
family (especially your faith family)?*

Even after reading this book; you can kick against it if
you want to (it's your choice after all), but you really don't
want God to get someone else because he'll let you live
long enough to see somebody else doing what you should
have been doing and HE WILL ERASE THE MEMORY
OF YOUR PARTICIPATION. None of us can (perhaps I
should say "should" because people do what they want!) do
what we want because we have been bought with a price.
The only way we can find fulfilment as human beings is to
find out what God has created us to do and then
passionately give ourselves to it. Remember, our
assignments as leaders have generational ramifications (and
I don't mean by human bloodlines alone!) and thus require

---

[112] Ditto P.22

generational participation. Therefore, Faith Resources teach, bless and send! Jesus established this pattern with His disciples. When you teach someone you establish your authority to lead them. The authority to lead is found in the ability to feed. Every time you send someone you establish the chain of command that exists within the structure. So teach them, send them, bless them!

> *Q: Did you know that to not purposefully plan to nor to not intentionally release each of your faith children; in a timely fashion, is to possess a "spider mentality" – 'I will die if I lose a leg/an arm"?*

However, the crucial paradigm shift that is required of this emerging new breed is one of a "starfish mentality" – 'If I lose a "leg"/an "arm"; not only will I regenerate it, but most importantly, the "lost" arm/leg will grow into a whole new starfish! Even if I risk "dying" by losing all my legs/arms, I am confident that at least 5 new starfish will emerge![113] This is the only mind-set/paradigm that is sure to possibly eradicate any *"Back-door Fear"*, [114]as well as prevent any actual back door activities or, indeed, any such clandestine moves.

---

[113] *"Starfish are famous for their ability to regenerate limbs, and in some cases, entire bodies… Some require the central body to be intact to regenerate, but a few spacies can grow an entirely new starfish just from a portion of a severed limb!"* – *animals.nationalgeographic.co.uk (accessed Monday 25/11/13).*
[114] Milan Ford, 26

*"Is it true that no matter where you go, it seems like everyone, these days, (some, more than others) is afraid of people "leaving"? Might it be an idea that instead of concentrating all our efforts on closing the **"back door"** maybe we should focus on opening **"the front"**! Did you know that when we refrain from teaching our people how and when to (properly) leave, we often endanger them, ourselves and indeed our organizations of becoming **lakes** (and possibly **swamps**) instead of **rivers?"***

Overall, with Faith Resources, nothing is impossible. Why? Because they operate in the realms of possibilities by simply ensuring that they do all that is necessary and needful as they stride in their destiny's call – all along functioning as destiny helpers to many. They are, in fact, kind of all things to all men that they might, by all means, win some to Christ. They are everything positive through Christ and shun every appearance of evil.[115]

Q: How will you decide to live and lead after reading this book?

---

[115] 1 Corinthians 9:22b (KJV)

This is a critical choice element that will determine your purpose and destiny in life:

1. Will you live and lead gain conscious? What can I get now? What's in it for me?

2. Will you live and lead greed conscious? Beyond what's in it for me right now, how do I maximise my leadership opportunities for the perpetual benefit of me and my immediate family, even beyond what is reasonable and sensible?

3. Will you live and lead God conscious, not being able to do anything without God i.e. forfeiting your own free will?[116]

Q: Is perfection possible for us "humans"? Are you a sinner or a saint? Do you consider yourself a sinner saved by grace or a saint who may sometimes falter or do you feel that there is no difference as these are just mere play of words? Does the dispensation of grace mean the abolition of decency, law and order?

Q: Who are you? What are you? Whose are you? Where are you?

---

[116] Sermon by Bishop I.V. Hilliard

Where you are right now is the starting point to the world! You can start here and go anywhere you want! Only you know your priorities, but one thing I do know is that people see what you are before they hear who or whose you are. What you are is revealed by what you do. What you do ultimately reveals what you believe. You will never leave where you are until you decide where you would rather be. So, stop looking at where you have been and start looking at where you can be. If God is your partner, you can afford to make big plans because although you cannot be what you are not, you can become what you are not![117]

Reach Your Potential: Charles W. Koller affirmed that through Christ you can be what you ought to be, do what you ought to do, and have what you ought to have (see Philippians 4:11, 13, 19), all to the glory of God. Therefore, I conclude by offering Christ to you as Lord and personal Saviour, if you are not born again.

If you are born again, I hope you have not just been inspired but also provoked to respond to my challenge to renew or upgrade your commitment in your walk and work with God and indeed the people around you. Your response to this *opportunity* determines who you are, what you are, whose you are and where you will ultimately be! Your answers and positive response reveal what you believe about yourself and the work God has called you to do as well as ensure that you not only emerge as a true Faith Resource but that you are also filled with the fullness

---

[117] Mike Murdock, 'One-Minute Pocket Bible – for the Business Professional' 2nd Printing (Tulsa, OK: Honour Books, 1994), P. 20, 24, 25 43, 117.

of God's glory – the Pleroma – wherefore you become truly resourceful!

Someone once said that the word POOR actually means Passing Over Opportunities Regularly

> Q: *Will you pass over this most important opportunity of your life yet AGAIN?*

Your decisions today will affect others tomorrow. Make the right choice! But ***'Sometimes we do not know what the lesson was until we have failed the test!'***[118]

> Q: *Did you understand the lesson? Could this call be the test? Will you make the right decisions and timely?*

You decide...

---

[118] Nelson's Quick Reference, 147

Conclusions

I *n the final analysis, it* is the author's ultimate hope and desire that the discussions, thoughts, ideas and concepts sparked in this book will engender a genuine quest for all Christians to aspire to emerge as true Faith Resources, wherein they become not just leaders or parents, or even just servant-leaders but ultimately become **parent-leaders** which encompasses everything (role, qualities etc.) that parenting and leadership in their respective rights, altogether, entail. This new concept of parent-leadership is the ultimate in leadership and parenting - simple but truly **transformational** and far-reaching in outcomes!

These emerging parent-leaders are essentially a new breed of Christians who understand and truly live out the principles of the sort of relational (also "three-dimensional) love that was initiated and continues to be demonstrated by God Himself. That necessary love of God that can do anything: make a way even where there isn't a way and knows that everything can start new every day. That same love that changed the whole world the moment it stepped in and knows that every day there are countless hearts to save, a world to win and that we can change lives, affirm divine callings and birth many destinies if we demonstrate such love to our faith children. These parent-leaders understand and truly live out the song-writer's charge - that love for our faith children will never and so should never pass away, and doesn't change from day-to-day depending on how we feel. It does not abandon, cut-off, nor destroy. Rather, it enduringly nurtures and builds.

If it's really love it just won't give up! But instead it necessarily walks through fire and flies higher each time. These parent-leaders have truly learnt this very same love from God our teacher – that love that is patient and kind, that love which knows that sometimes we necessarily have to lose in order to win, that love that believes and trusts in our faith children, that love that forgives, that love that doesn't mind if someone else wins. God is indeed the start of all of this and parent-leaders know and strive to do the same – giving no excuses, just results!

When we attain this mark as Christians, we will see that in all areas of our endeavors, we will be driven by compassion, not obsession and all our actions will be rooted in relationships, not systems and we will promote life, not self-image.

If we fail in these areas much of what we do (mostly disparately) as parents and leaders will eventually be blown away. The parent-leader is what the new breed looks like and that is the ultimate Faith Resource - the future and the very will of God!

Q: Did you know that Parent-Leaders are Christians who also possess PATIENCE & REFLECTION in their "wisdom-tool-kit". Patience: the weapon that forces deception to reveal itself. Reflection: the tool that turns experience into insight?

Prayer Points And Prophetic Declarations

*T*ake a moment to reflect upon and then review your life, ministry, walk and work with God so far, as well as your relationships and connections. Repent/make amends where necessary, count your blessings and thank God for His patience, grace, mercies and faithfulness and determine to extend bowels of these to others. Then make the following declarations and prayers:

1. Father, I forthwith dedicate/rededicate to you my entire life/existence/all that concerns me - home, ministry, business, relationships, children, gifts, abilities, resources etc.

2. I declare that my spirit is hereby liberated to follow your Spirit. Lord arise, therefore, and uproot whatever seeds you did not plant inside me in Jesus's name.

3. By the workings of the Holy Spirit, I hereby declare my eyes open to see beyond the visible into the invisible and that I am henceforth fortified to emerge as a new breed with divine power for the next level, in Jesus's name.

4. I declare that the Lord has equipped me for service. I prophesy and decree my immediate and automatic miraculous location in the place of my service, fulfilment, breakthroughs and ultimate destiny, in Jesus's name.

5. I declare that the Lord has, forthwith, impregnated me with His agenda for my life and ministry. Therefore I decree and declare the full counsel of God. Both His decision and pronouncement oracles are to take full effect in my life, in Jesus's name.[119]

6. Lord, I receive, now! Your Spirit of discernment and wisdom to recognise opportunities and the divine enablement to act accordingly so as to maximise every moment of my life in Jesus's name.

7. I decree for myself that divine direction will propel my life into greatness with the mandate to enter into covenant of wealth, anointing to discern God's perfect will and divine purpose for my life. I am hereby miraculously catapulted into greatness that will bring cataclysmic confusion in the enemies' camps even like Daniel in the land of Babylon and like Mordecai, in Jesus's name!

8. Every strongman delegated to confuse me is hereby bound. I see the Lord dispatching angels to roll every stumbling block against my destiny and I hereby bind and cast out the spirits of disobedience, insincerity and selfishness from my life. I hereby decree that I am subject to the Spirit of the living God to quicken my whole being in the direction of

---

[119] Decision oracles are God's direct response when we ask him a question or seek His counsel. Pronouncement oracles are God's word to a situation or a person even though no word from God had been sought" – Holman Bible Dictionary page 1225

my destiny, purpose and function as a true Faith Resource in Jesus's name.

9. I confess and decree that I am that tree planted by the rivers of living water. Everything I do shall prosper in Jesus's name. My fruit shall be for food and my leaf for healing, in Jesus's name! (see Ezekiel 47:12)

10.I declare that I am not just a Faith Resource, I am indeed resourceful! I am indeed a river and not a lake nor a swamp! I am a channel of blessing, I will bear fruit, I declare that God had indeed granted me good success and I am truly successful in Jesus's name. I will bear the true marks of success i.e. successors, spiritual children etc. in Jesus's name. I hear God saying to me, 'Well done, my good and faithful servant, enter into my rest for you have done well.' If you heard that, say a befitting 'AMEN!'

God bless, keep and cover you under the shadow of His wings and may all the glory, honour, dominion, power, majesty and praise be His for ever and ever and ever. AMEN!

WARNING:EXTREMELY IMPORTANT NOTE BEFORE YOU PROCEED ANY FURTHER!!

Writer John Bunyan reminds us that: "you have not lived today until you have done something for someone who can never repay you."[120] That is a matter of your attitude & response to God's call (even through this book) to the ultimate level of service – that of Parent-Leadership.

So, what's your attitude here: Are you choosing to serve or are you choosing to be a servant?

*When we choose to merely serve we are still in charge. We decide whom we will serve and when we will serve. But when we choose to be a servant, this is a deliberately different attitude in our choice to serve wherefore we give up the right to be in charge. We become **available and vulnerable!** This ultimate level of servanthood/servant-leadership leads not to a sense of duty but to an expression of love. This discipline of service becomes a means of experiencing God's grace in finding/obtaining and expressing His wisdom. This is the litmus test for every Faith Resource who is truly a Parent-Leader.[121]*

*Therefore, if your answer is that you are choosing to serve rather than choosing to be a servant (in service), if you are here out of duty rather than out of love – even the love for wisdom – and your genuine desire to do better; then I would ask, "What are you doing here!" and exclaim with Scripture: **"What is this? Fools out shopping for wisdom! They wouldn't recognise it if they saw it!**[122] I urge you to please either drop this book right away! Or quite simply go back and re-read this book and ensure that you understand the lessons so far.*

But if you answered in the correct affirmative, then by all-means do proceed to enter this final chapter with much excitement and expectation....

---

[120] John Bunyan (Author of 'The Pilgrim's Progress'), www.goodreads.com . Also see Luke 14:12-14 (NIV)
[121] Richard J. Foster, 'Celebration of Discipline: The Path to Spiritual Growth', (USA: HarperCollins, 1998).
[122] Proverbs 17:16 (MSG).

Wise Quotables

hankfully, I realised relatively early in my life that wisdom is the only real need I will ever have. So, throughout my life, along the paths of my faith journey and in my strides of destiny, I have passionately pursued it! I have thus been impacted by many inspiring and truly challenging wise words. In the same vein I have had moments of great revelation in counselling many with words of wisdom that I knew were not beforehand in my repertoire of knowledge; words that have helped me and many others in diverse situations. Some of these words are novel to me as received in my moments of divine inspiration, others have been collated or culled from my various readings, encounters and experiences.

As a bonus, I have chosen to share some of these thought-provoking words that God has given to me personally, as well as some from other great people of God. These are some of the words that I have carried with me and that have helped me and many others immensely along the paths and strides of our destinies, and I hope will help you too:

⬩ The first step to success is the willingness to listen. Cultivate a teachable spirit. *Culled from The Pocket Bible.*

⬩ You only live once, but if you work it right, once is enough. Be a true worshipper. True worship is not forced past. It's an unavoidable intimacy (a lifestyle), in fact your life! It's the love room where your future is born. *The Pocket Bible.*

✦ Your future is determined by your ability to follow instructions! God will not advance you beyond your last act of obedience. The ability to follow is the first qualification for leadership. *The Pocket Bible.*

✦ Prosperity is having enough of God's provision to complete His instructions for your life. *The Pocket Bible.*

✦ A man would do nothing if he waited until he could do it so well that no one could find fault. *John Henry Cardinal Newman.*

✦ All men fall. The great ones get back up! *The Pocket Bible.*

✦ Losers focus on what they are going through while champions focus on what they are going to. Winners are just ex-losers who got 'mad'. *The Pocket Bible.*

✦ If you don't change the way you live you will die the way you live. *Eze.*

✦ Those who do not respect your time will not respect your wisdom either. *The Pocket Bible.*

✦ Go where you are celebrated not where you are tolerated. *The Pocket Bible.*

✦ What you fail to destroy in your life will eventually destroy you. *The Pocket Bible.*

✦ Discontent is the catalyst for change. Intolerance of the present creates a future. *The Pocket Bible.*

✦ Sometimes we do not know what the lesson was until we have failed the test! *Warren W. Wiersbe.*

✦ Decisions. We make them. Then they turn around and make us. And sometimes they break us! *Alice Mathews*.

✦ Your decisions today will affect others tomorrow. Make the right decisions! *Warren W. Wiersbe*.

✦ You are not in business until you've done business with the Father. Do business with the FATHER today! – *Eze*.

✦ When God strips away your resources, it is not to impoverish your life but to enrich your faith. *Warren W. Wiersbe*.

✦ Money is a wonderful servant, a terrible master, and abominable god. *Warren W. Wiersbe*.

✦ Some study the exit of every penny, others study the entry of every dollar. The wise do both. *The Pocket Bible*.

✦ Make all you can, save all you can, give all you can. *John Wesley*.

✦ For it's in giving that we receive. *St. Francis of Assisi*.

✦ Not 'how did he die?' but 'how did he live?' Not 'what did he gain?' but 'what did he give?'. *Author unknown*.

✦ Mercy is like money. Your deposits determine your withdrawal. (*see Matthew 5:7 & 6:15*).

✦ Crisis always occurs at the curve of change and satan always attacks those next in line for a promotion – new levels, new devils! *Eze*.

✦ There is a 'peace' that is worse than war! *Eze*.

✤ Pain is discomfort created by disorder. It is not your enemy, but merely the proof that one exists. *The Pocket Bible.*

✤ Peace is not the absence of conflict; it's the absence of inner conflict. *The Pocket Bible.*

✤ Great peace have they who love your law, and nothing can make them stumble. (*Psalm 119:165*).

✤ Learn to do business in the place of prayer, it is most profitable. *Eze.*

✤ When God wants to bless you, He puts a 'person' in your life. Those who created yesterday's pain do not control tomorrow's potential. God never consults your past to determine your future. Although sometimes you may be required to go back in order to move forward! *Eze.*

✤ You want to see a miracle? Be the miracle! You are the seed that decides the harvest around you. *Eze.*

✤ We should (therefore) seek not so much to pray but to become prayer. *St. Francis of Assisi.*

✤ It's the seed which grows, the yeast which spreads, the mustard seed which skyrockets, and the net which draws the fish. All the workers need to do is sow, throw, mix and wait. It's both easy and terribly difficult (all at once!). *Phil Moore.*

✤ It may take courage to hunt on the back of a lion but it takes common sense to know when to run away. *Author unknown.*

✤ Never rewrite your theology to accommodate a desire.

⚓ He that goeth forth and weepeth, bearing precious seed shall doubtless come again with rejoicing, bringing his sheaves with him. *Psalm 126:6.*

⚓ Acting and behaving like a Christian and you are not? Well keep on acting; for you might just become a Christian soon! Then you will act and behave like a Christian because you are a Christian! *Eze.*

⚓ Those in high places can be brought down. Those in low places can be called up. Humility is the awareness of it. *The Pocket Bible.*

⚓ Children are likely to live up to what you believe of them. *Lady Bird Johnson.*

⚓ You don't raise heroes, you raise sons. And if you treat them like sons, they'll turn out to be heroes, even if it's just in your own eyes. *Walter Schirra.*

⚓ Never complain about what you permit. *The Pocket Bible.*

⚓ Example is not the most important matter in influencing others – it is the only matter. *Albert Schweitzer.*

⚓ We all have weaknesses. But I have thought that others have put up with mine so tolerantly that I would be less than fair not to make a reasonable discount for theirs. *William Allen White.*

⚓ You can't hold a man down without staying down with him. *Booker T. Washington.*

⚓ The father only builds, never destroys. *Douglas MacArthur.*

🔱 Children are the living messages we will send to a time we will not see. *John Whitehead.*

🔱 An amicable man is one who listens with a smile to what he already knows, told by a person who doesn't. *Alfred Capus.*

🔱 A small man stands on others. A great man stands on God. *John Mason.*

🔱 There is only one job opening in the Church - 'Servants'! *TD Jakes.*

🔱 Preparation for spiritual leadership takes time. When God selects you for a task, no excuses are acceptable. *Jim George.*

🔱 Give no excuses, just results! *Eze*

🔱 Those who think ahead, get ahead. *Anonymous.*

🔱 What doesn't get measured doesn't get treasured. *Anonymous.*

🔱 What's measured improves. *Peter Drucker.*

🔱 Not 'what was his station?' but 'had he a heart?' and 'how did he play his God-given part?' These are the units to measure the worth of a man, regardless of birth. *Anonymous.*

🔱 What we count as important influences our attitude and the views we hold and affects our behaviour and how we act and react to what we encounter. *Anonymous.*

✦ Forgiveness: sometimes the only way to win is to lose. Have you been to the street called Straight? (*See Acts 9:11*) *Eze.*

✦ Gratitude is simply awareness of the givers in your life. You cannot name one thing that was not given to you. *The Pocket Bible.*

✦ Winners do not like to lose, but winners are not afraid of losing. *Prof. Willie Rilo.*

✦ Champions make decisions that create the future they desire while losers make decisions that create the present they desire. Champions are willing to do things they hate, to create something they love. *The Pocket Bible.*

✦ The greatest lesson in life is to know that even fools are right sometimes. *Winston Churchill.*

✦ A little nonsense now and then is relished by even the wisest of men. *Anonymous.*

✦ Parenting: The lines between biological and the spirit ought to be cleared by the Spirit. *Eze.*

✦ Singles/unmarried: **Do not "DO" until you say, "I DO".** *Eze.*

✦ Power is the ability to walk away from something you desire to protect something you love. What you are willing to walk away from determines what God will bring to you. *The Pocket Bible.*

✦ We always seem better at and indeed far more interested in spotting mistakes, but would you purpose to catch someone doing something right today? *Eze.*

⊣ To develop positive, successful people, look for the gold, not the dirt. *John C. Maxwell.*

⊣ Not he is great that can alter matter, but he that can alter my state of mind. *Ralph Waldo Emerson.*[123]

⊣ Leading leaders lead leaders – teach them, send them, bless them! *Eze.*

⊣ Satan's favourite entry point into your life is always through someone close to you. *The Pocket Bible.*

⊣ Sometimes it's necessary to go back in order to move forward. *Eze.*

⊣ The broken become masters at mending. *The Pocket Bible.*

⊣ What you make happen for others God will make happen for you. *The Pocket Bible.*

⊣ You will be remembered in life by the problems you solve and the problems you create, as well as the pain or the pleasures you have created. Your success is determined by the problems you solve for others and for these you'll be pursued. The problem that infuriates you the most is the problem God has assigned you to solve. *The Pocket Bible.*

⊣ Money is merely a reward for solving problems. Wealth is when you have a lot of something you love. Your success is determined by the problems you solve for others. If you simply love helping people and solving problems, you will naturally have plenty of money! *Eze.*

---

[123] Nanus, 23

If what you say to someone cannot be said to everyone, or at least to the one of whom you speak, then say it to no one but God! *Eze.*

Your assignment is decided by God and discovered by you. It is geographical and is always to a person or people. It is always to solve a problem for someone. Currents of favour begin to flow the moment you solve a problem for someone. Those who unlock your compassion are those to whom you have been assigned. *The Pocket Bible.*

Never give more time to a critic than you would give to a friend. Never discuss your problem with someone who cannot solve it. **Silence cannot be misquoted.** *The Pocket Bible.*

Do not make friends with a hot-tempered man, do not associate with one easily angered. Do not go to your brother's house in the day of your calamity; better a neighbour nearby than a brother far away. (*See Prov. 22:24a, 27:6,9,10*).

Those who will lie for you will certainly lie to you and, eventually, lie about you. Those who will sin with you will eventually sin against you. *The Pocket Bible.*

Parent-Leaders are those who also possess PATIENCE & REFLECTION in their "wisdom-tool-kit". Patience: the weapon that forces deception to reveal itself; and reflection: the tool that turns experience into insight.

Select Bibliography
Books

Abam, W. Israel: *Strides of Destiny – Lessons From The Attitudes of Moses*, (Migeria, Abuja: LightGuide Publishing, 2011).

Bunton, Peter, 'Cell Groups and House Churches - What History Teaches Us' (Lititz, Pannsylvania; House to House Publications, 2001

Chapman, Gary: *The Five Love Languages*, (Chicago: Northfield Publishing, 2007) – Edited by Tracey D. Lawrence.

Edwars, Gene: *A Tale of Three Kings – A Study in Brokenness*, (Newman, Georgia: SeedSowers, 1992).

Ford, Milan: *83 Things I Wish The Black Church Would Stop Doing*, (USA: ThePewView.com, 2009).

Foster, J. Richard, 'Celebration of Discipline: The Path to Spiritual Growth', (USA: HarperCollins, 1998).

Grenz, Stanley J. & Olson, Roger E., *'Who Needs Theology? An Invitation to the Study of God'* (Leicester, England: InterVarsity Press, 1996)

Hughes, John: *The Pastor's Notebook*, (Eastbourne, England: Kingsway Publication, 2003).

Idleman, Kyle: *Not a Fan – Becoming a Completely Committed Follower of Jesus*, (Grand Rapids, MI: Zondervan, 2011).

Kreider, Larry: *'The Cry for Spiritual Fathers & Mothers – Compelling Vision for Authentic, Nurturing Relationships Within Today's Church,* (Ephara, PA: House to House Publication, 2000)

Lucado, Max: *Just Like Jesus*,(Nashville: Word Publishing, 1998).

Lutzer, Erwin: *Pastor to Pastor: Tackling the Problems of Ministry'*, (Grand Rapids, MI: Kregel Publications, 1998).

Maxwell, John C.: *Developing the Leaders Around You*, (Nashville, Tennessee: Thomas Nelson, 1995).

Maxwell, John C.: *The 21 Irrefutable Laws of Leadership – Follow Them and People Will Follow You.* (Nashville, Tennessee: Thomas Nelson, 1998 and 2007).

Mills, San-Mari (Compiler): *Life's Little Book For Fathers* (Hong Kong: Christian Art, 1998).

Miskell, Jane R. and Miskell Vincent: *Motivation At Work*, (New York: IRWIN, 1994).

Murdock, Mike: *One-Minute Pocket Bible – for the Business Professional*, 2nd Printing (Tulsa, OK: Honor Books, 1994).

Nanus, Burt, Dobbs, M. Stephen: *Leaders Who Make A Difference – Essential Strategies For Meeting The Nonprofit Challenge*, (San Francisco: Josey-Bass Publishers, 1999).

Onwubuiko, C. Moses: *James: Faith Without Works is Dead – An Urgent Call to Practical Christianity.* (Ontario Canada: Essence Publishing, 2011).

Page, Nick: *The Big Story – what actually happens in the Bible* (London, UK: Authentic Media, 2007).

Peterson, H. Eugene: *The Book of Proverbs – The Message,* (Colourado: NAVPRESS, 2004).

Standing, Roger, 'Re-emerging Church – Strategies for Reaching a Returning Generation' (UK: BRF- Bible Reading Fellowship, 2008).

Thomas, Viv: *Future Leader,* (Cumbria: Paternoster Press, 2001).

Wilson, Friensen & Paulson (Joint Authors): *Restoring The Fallen – A Team Approach To Caring, Confronting & Reconciling,* (Downers Grove, Illinois: InterVersity Press, 1997).

Wogu, Christian: *Building a Stronger Economy – My Dream For My Country,* (Lagos: El-TODA Ventures for Shechinah Resources, 2010).

Bibles

Burgraph, Mark, *Mantis Bible Study (KJV),* (v 4.9.4, www.mantisbible.com)

Hebrew-Greek Key Word Study Bible (KJV), (USA: AMG Publishers, 1991)

Hayford, W. Jack, *Spirit Filled Life Bible For Students (NKJV)*, (London: Thomas Nelson Publishers, 1995)

Extreme Teen Bible (NKJV), (USA: Thomas Nelson Publishers, 1999)

Commentaries, Concordances & Other Materials

Bible Handbook (Nashville: Thomas Nelson, 1995)

Bible Concordance (NKJV), (Nashville: Thomas Nelson, 1999)

George, Jim, 'The Bare Bones Bible Handbook', (Oregon: Harvester House
Publishers, 2006)

Mathew Henry's Commentary, (Michigan: Zondervan, 1961)

Strong, James, Strong's Exhaustive Concordance of The Bible, (London: Thomas Nelson Publishers, 1990)

Wiersbe, W. Warren, 'Nelson's Quick Reference Chapter-By-Chapter Bible Commentary (Nashville: Thomas Nels/.on, 1991)

Dictionaries

Collins Softback English Dictionary, (Great Britain: HarperCollins Publishers, 1992)

Holman Illustrated Bible Dictionary, (Nashville: Holman Bible Publishers, 2003)

Mounce, D. Williams, 'Mounce's Complete Expository Dictionary of Old & New Testament Words', (Michigan: Zondervan, 2006)

Zondervan Compact Bible Dictionary, (Michigan: Zondervan, 1993)